Dr. Ian C. B. Pearce
BA, BM, B.Ch, MRCS, LRCP

THE HOLISTIC
APPROACH TO CANCER

SAFFRON WALDEN
THE C. W. DANIEL COMPANY LIMITED

First published in Great Britain
by R. Findlay, Boturich, Alexandria, Dumbartonshire

This edition published by
The C.W. Daniel Company Limited
1 Church Path, Saffron Walden
Essex, CB10 1JP, England

Reprinted 1995

ISBN 0 85207 211 2

The Random House Group Limited supports The Forest Stewardship
Council (FSC®), the leading international forest certification organisation.
Our books carrying the FSC label are printed on FSC® certified paper.
FSC is the only forest certification scheme endorsed by the leading
environmental organisations, including Greenpeace. Our
paper procurement policy can be found at
www.randomhouse.co.uk/environment

Set in 11/12pt Bembo by MS Typesetting,
Castle Camps, Cambridge

MIX
Paper | Supporting
responsible forestry
FSC
www.fsc.org   FSC® C018179

Printed and bound in Great Britain by Clays Ltd, St Ives PLC

Readers are encouraged to join New Approaches to Cancer (NAC) and obtain the periodical *Harmony*, to keep in touch with the latest developments. The annual fee helps to support NAC, and further donations and legacies are needed. The address is:

New Approaches to Cancer
5 Larksfield
Egham
Surrey
TW20 0RB
England
Telephone: 01784 433610

Contents

Preface

Statistics show that about one in four persons are likely to develop cancer during their life time, and that, next to cardiovascular disease, cancer is the commonest cause of death among the western democracies. Despite the expenditure of millions of pounds on research, the overall figures for recovery from the three major forms of cancer in the west — breast cancer, bowel cancer, and lung cancer — have shown very little improvement over the past 40 years. Those forms of cancer in which the figures for recovery do show some improvement with modern medical technology — such as skin cancer and some cancers of the blood and reproductive organs — form only a small proportion of the overall incidence of the disease.

While great advances have been made in understanding the cancerous process at the cellular level, the traditional approach has shown little understanding of the processes which precede the development of the cancerous lesion, or those which appear to determine the variations in response to therapy between different persons with the same type of cancer. In other words, while advances have been made in understanding the 'how', little is understood of the 'why' of cancer.

Traditional medicine persists in regarding the cancer tumour as a disease in its own right, and bends all its therapeutic efforts towards the eradication of the tumour, instead of viewing the tumour as the indicator — or symptom — of a generalised disorder of body physiology. Thus, while often strikingly successful in dealing with the primary tumour, conventional therapy leaves the underlying process untouched, with the

3

consequent development of later recurrences through the continuing operation of the causative process.

Statistics show that about 1 in 100,000 cancers regress spontaneously, and that many other persons, dying from causes other than cancer are found at post mortem to have deposits of cancerous cells within their bodies, which are being perfectly well contained by the body, with no symptoms of cancer. The number of these considerably exceeds the number of those who actually develop cancer. This suggests that the body has its own methods of dealing with cancerous cells. It is further known that the artificial suppression of the immune rejection mechanism, such as takes place in the case of organ transplants, results in a higher incidence of cancer among the recipients of such transplants (2.4 – 4 times higher according to the type of cancer). It would therefore seem likely that studies of this naturally occurring protective mechanism, and of the reasons for its apparent breakdown in persons who develop cancer, would be of the highest value both in the actual management of cancer, and in the protection of the community from developing cancer.

Studies for the life histories of persons developing cancer have shown that three out of every four of these have been subjected during the two or three years preceding the development of their cancer to severe emotional stress of a very particular type. These include bereavement, retirement, redundancy, migration, dispersal of families and so on. Furthermore, many of these people have been brought up in a state of emotional isolation in early childhood, have difficulties in forming close personal relationships, and are very reserved in the expression of their emotions, especially those of resentment, guilt, hostility, hurt and grief. Many also, while leading lives of selfless devotion to the needs of others, fail to pay sufficient attention to the satisfaction of their own inner psychological needs — or even to recognise that they have any such needs. Many, too, adopt a 'victim' stance towards the reverses of life, and, meeting these with feelings of helplessness and hopelessness, have few inner resources upon which to fall back when faced with severe emotional challenge. Lacking any knowledge of the inner, self-healing power of their bodies, and of the ways in which these can be mobilised and reinforced by themselves, they have little inner compulsion to fight the disease, and prefer to hand over the problems to the skill and expertise of the professionals.

The new approach to cancer seeks to teach patients — and doctors — how these self-healing powers can be reinforced, both through correct body maintenance by proper nutrition, and through the correction of faulty and negative attitudes towards life and towards their disease. Techniques of biofeedback have shown that a vast range of body functions, hitherto not thought to be susceptible to control by the mind, can in fact be influenced by mental processes carried out in a deeply relaxed state. Patients are therefore instructed in methods of deep relaxation, including meditation and auto- genic training, and how to visualise self-healing taking place. This is designed, with counselling and psychotherapy, to help patients to move away from attitudes of despair and hopelessness towards a positive belief in recovery, and to change whatever patterns of negative thought may have been present prior to the development of the cancer. Patients are also advised about correct nutrition, and provided with diet sheets and a schedule of vitamin and mineral supplements designed to assist in the correct operation of the immune system.

It must be clearly understood that these methods of dealing with cancer are **not** to be considered as an alternative to the methods of traditional medicine. They must be seen as working alongside the orthodox approach, and extending it into areas which it has so far been unable or unwilling, to penetrate. What is required is not the substitution of orthodox treatment by the new methods, but rather a marriage of the two approaches, so that patients can be helped on levels other than the purely physical. So far the rather one-eyed stance of orthodoxy has precluded these methods from systematic evaluation, and very few cancer clinics are prepared to take them seriously. Various reasons are put forward for this, including lack of space and funding in the hospital programme. Another reason for the current lack of enthusiasm may be the unwillingness of patients in general to become involved in their own healing processes.

(Dr Bernard Siegel, of New Haven, Connecticut, found only 12 out of a total of 100 patients responded to his invitation to heal themselves.) Most of the work that is being done in this field is being done by private individuals, who lack the sophisticated means of monitoring, available to large clinics, and who are thus restricted to purely empirical observations. While it is still much too early to claim that these methods constitute a definitive approach to the problem of cancer, it should at least be possible to set up a number of pilot schemes at selected cancer clinics at which they might be properly evaluated. If proper evaluation is to take place, such an approach needs to be employed from the outset of the disease, instead of, as is happening now in so many instances, as the last resort of the destitute, for whom orthodoxy has nothing more to offer. Patients should receive counselling and nutritional advice **before** they come for surgery, and not, as generally happens now, when chemotherapy has failed, and the immune system has no further powers of resistance.

New Approaches to Cancer seeks through a programme of continued education, both of the general public, and of the medical profession, to exert pressure for the development and more general employment of these new methods. Persons interested are invited to apply to become members, and thus help in the furtherance of the development of a new climate in cancer therapy. New Approaches to Cancer is a registered charity (No. 285530), and will welcome the support of all who read these pages.

Cancer and You

When people are told that they have cancer, they are apt to feel shocked, angry and frightened. They usually still have the idea that they have 'caught' a fatal disease, and, unless it has been found early on, that they will inevitably slip towards death within a measurable period of a few years or even a few months. Furthermore, most patients still think that only the doctors can help them, and tend to assume that even this help is regrettably limited. For most patients have not yet heard of a very different idea about the nature of cancer and its cure, which is now gaining ground.

You have been told that you have cancer. **There is a great deal you can do to help yourself. You have a good chance of reversing your cancer. Take courage!**

You have to attack it on two levels, and really **work** at it. First, know that your own attitude is crucial. Like a voodoo victim, if you expect to die, you may well assist the event. If you don't expect to die, you take the first step in your return to health. So when you have read this, get started on your belief system right away, and that of those around you.

You are an important person, a worthwhile person. Your personal needs and desires are important and must be taken seriously. If you are to return to health, they have to be met if possible. Try to live in an atmosphere of serene harmony, and don't let others get you down. Your own relaxed and peaceful mind is the most important thing in your life right now. Those around you can help or hinder you in your task; enlist their aid.

Cancer is a dis-ease of the whole person — spirit, mind and emotions — as well as body. Probably most of us have cancer cells in our bodies from time to time; perhaps all the time. But

7

our bodies are able to contain and destroy these cells and stop them running wild. In cancer patients, the body defence system has broken down, just as it does when we get a bad cold. We take too little care to keep this defence system running efficiently. We interfere with it, partly through incorrect feeding, partly through our emotional and mental attitudes and habits. (How often does one hear of cancer appearing after an emotional accident, or a series of shocks which a person has had difficulty in handling? And how striking is this century's rise in cancer in modern western societies who live increasingly on processed and preserved foods.)

So here is your task: an attack on two levels, to allow the body's defence system to return to full working order, and so bring about a restoration of wholeness and health.

LEVEL ONE: Get started on right eating. Our western diet is an open door to cancer, with its high proportion of manufactured foodstuffs and additives. Try to eat lots of **uncooked** vegetables and fruit, and as fresh as possible and organically grown if possible; 'garden to gullet' in one short move. Sprouting grains and seeds help here, with pulses for protein, and nuts. Include the minimum of dairy produce, and keep right off meat in the early stages. Get on to this routine **right away**, and stay with it. Keep off the following, which prevent your return to health: tobacco, tea, coffee, chocolate, alcohol, opium-derived drugs, fluoridised or other forms of treated water (fresh spring water is best, Volvic or Spa mineral waters are particularly recommended), animal protein, sugar, white flour and processed foods. Drink three or four glasses of carrot juice every day (which helps to attack the cancer cells), with a little safflower oil or fresh cream whisked up to aid absorption. Take large doses of vitamin C; up to 10 to 15 grammes every day.

Further dietary advice is included herein.

LEVEL TWO: Learn about deep relaxation. Learn about methods of deep relaxation/meditation/visualisation, and start to practise this daily: three 15 minute periods every day without fail. It neutralises stress in mind and body and helps to restore harmony throughout your whole being. You can order cassette tapes about this from New Approaches to Cancer.

No one can promise a cure. What can be said is that a growing number of people have pulled themselves round by these methods, taking the responsibility for their health upon themselves. Some have appeared on television to say so. This is **not** an alternative to orthodox therapy; it is complementary to it, and greatly enhances its effects. It is extending orthodox therapy into areas which it does not usually reach at present.

You **can** improve the quality of your life, and give the restorative healing forces a better chance to accomplish their task. **So get started on it right away**.

Glossary

adrenals: secretory glands, situated on top of the kidneys.

analgesics: pain-relieving drugs.

atheroma: the deposition of fatty substances in the lining of the arteries, thereby leading to narrowing of the artery.

carcinoma: a form of cancer.

carcinogenic: cancer producing.

chronic: persisting over a period of time.

cutaneous: to do with the skin.

cytotoxic: poisonous to cells.

cytotoxins: chemical substances employed in therapy to kill cancer cells; usually administered by injection or by mouth.

epidemiology: the study of the spread of disease, with especial reference to the reasons associated with its spread.

genes: hereditary factors, present in the nucleus of every cell, which interact with the environment to produce the characters of the organism. They control, amongst other things, the growth and development of the cell in which they are present.

genetic: carried on the genes; genetic characteristics are inherited from the parent and carried on the genes of the cell.

hysterectomy: the operation of surgical removal of the womb.

laryngectomy: the operation of surgical removal of the larynx.

lymphocytes: certain of the white blood corpuscles.

T-lymphocytes or T-cells: white blood corpuscles originating in the thymus gland.

mastectomy: the operation of surgical removal of the breast.

macrophages: large white cells, present in the blood, whose function is the destruction of abnormal cells, and 'foreign' invaders in the body. (Gr. *macros* large; *phagein* to devour).

metabolism: body chemistry.

metabolic: to do with body chemistry.

metastasis: remote spread of cancer to other areas.

morbidity: tendency to develop disease.

naturopathy: the treatment of disease by natural means; not medicines.

oncology: the study of cancer.

oncological: to do with the study of cancer.

oncologist: a doctor specialising in the treatment of cancer, usually by means of radiation or chemotherapy.

pathogen: a disease-producing organism or substance.

prognosis: the probable outcome of a disease.

psyalomucin: a type of chemical compound found in the body; it forms the basis of a protective sheath surrounding cancer cells, which tends to protect them against the working of the immune system.

psychogenic: originating with the mind or emotions.

renal: to do with the kidneys.

steroids: chemical substances secreted by the adrenal cortex.

symbiosis: living together in close association in the body, without interfering with each other.

toxic: poisonous.

toxins: poisins.

CHAPTER I

The Holistic Approach

"The cure of a part should not be attempted without treatment of the whole. No attempt should be made to cure the body without the soul, and therefore, if the head and body are to be healthy, you must begin by curing the mind. That is the first thing. Let no one persuade you to cure the head until he has first given you his soul to be cured. For this is the great error of our day in the treatment of the human body, that physicians first separate the soul from the body." *Plato.*

Plato's words, written over two and a half thousand years ago, are as true today as they were in those far-off times. In no field of medical endeavour is this more so than in the field of cancer, where the truly holistic approach is so desperately needed if the shadow of incipient death is ever to be lifted from this terrible disease, and mankind released from the fear and hopelessness which seem inevitably to accompany it. This paper in no way attempts to cover the whole field of the holistic approach to cancer, which is now finding increasingly wide acceptance amongst patients, if not amongst doctors, on both sides of the Atlantic. It is, rather, an account of a personal approach, and of the thinking which led up to it. It is the belief of the writer that this is worthy of a somewhat wider application and evaluation than it is at present receiving, and that proper comparisons of its efficacy as compared with that of unaided orthodox therapy should be made without delay, in an attempt to improve the success rate of treatment among patients with cancer.

The word *holism* is used to express the concept that *the whole is greater than the sum of its parts*, and the term *holistic* to mean the application of this concept. It embodies the view of post-Einsteinian physics that the reality of any object or creature consists not in the individual properties of the creature or object, but rather in the inter-relationships, interconnections and interactions with one another, both of the component parts within the creature or object, and of the creature or object itself with other creatures or objects in the surrounding environment. (Examples of the truth of this concept can be seen both amongst the cells and organs of the body itself, and among the units of the family, the community, the nations of the world and the ecology of the planet.)

Such a concept is in stark contrast to the current views of most of the orthodox section of the medical profession, and of much of western science, whose thinking is contained within the Cartesian dictum that *the whole is the sum of its parts.* In accordance with this view it then becomes necessary to understand the whole by breaking it down into its component parts, analysing these, and then attempting to put it together again from an understanding of those parts. The whole of the current western medical model is founded upon this concept. In this, each organism is viewed in terms of its parts — both cells and organs — and its properties are considered to be those of the aggregation of those of the component parts. In accordance with this view, medical students make their first investigations into the human organism via the dissection room and the physiology laboratory, and learn to look upon the human organism as a collection of cells and organs. Such a system is a reductionist system and its thinking is mechanistic and materialistic. It has resulted in the concept that the body is to be viewed as a machine, ever prone to breakdown unless supervised and serviced by experts all the time, and this concept has now been extended into attempts to introduce spare parts into the machine. Descartes, the eighteenth century philosopher actually spoke of *Le Bête Machine*, (the animal as a machine), and in 1928 Joseph Needham, the Cambridge philosopher, wrote: "In science, man is a machine: or if he is not, he is nothing." In this view, disease is looked upon as an accidental happening, occurring at random from without, and the healing of that disease is considered to be the result of intervention from without. The inevitable consequence of this approach has been the growth of our present system of high cost, technologically oriented medicine, with the patient becoming ever more and more a mere cypher in the hands of the experts, with little or no involvement in the procedure adopted to heal his disease. In the United Kingdom, in particular, this approach has been powerfully reinforced by a state system of medicine, which both denies room for true communication between doctors and patients, and removes responsibility for health care from the individual patient, and vests it in an all-powerful professional caste.

Holism, on the other hand, views the organism as a web of inter-relationships, inter-connections and interactions, both within itself, with the surrounding environment, and with other organisms contained within that environment. Furthermore, the environment is considered to include not merely the immediate physical environment, but also the psychological environment, embracing both past and future, as well as the present, together with the cultural, sociological, ecological and last but by no means least, spiritual and cosmic environment. The organism is further viewed as being composed of a number of separate and interacting planes of energy: material, electrical, emotional, psychical and spiritual planes. The healthy organism is considered to be in a state of balance both within and between the various planes of energy. This system of balanced energy is homoeostatic: that is to say if the balance has become disturbed, there is a natural tendency to return spontaneously to a state of balance, once the disturbing force has been neutralised or removed. Disease is considered to be the manifestation at a physical level of a state of imbalance existing either within or between the various energy planes, or between the energy planes of the creature and those comprising the environment. Put in simpler terms, this means that there is within each creature an innate power of self-healing, which operates, **unless interfered with or destroyed**, to restore health. The task of the doctor or healer is considered to be the recognition of a state of imbalance, whether actual or incipient, and assistance to the organism, either by triggering off, or by providing the optimum conditions for, the operation of the mechanism for the regaining of balance once it has been lost.

The holistic approach to healing rests upon four major principles:

1. The patient exists on a variety of levels, all of which are of equal importance. He must be considered as an **individual** on **all** of them. In helping a person to be healed of disease, we should ideally operate on as many of these levels as is possible at any one time. This means that there is no such thing as an *alternative approach*. There are adjunctive or complementary methods of therapy, but no single method is complete in itself.

2. The patient has within him self-healing and self-repair systems, which must be regarded as crucial in both the prevention and treatment of illness. It is important that this never be lost sight of, and that all methods of therapy employed are prevented from damaging this all-important mechanism. C.f. the ancient maxim *Primum est non nocere* (the first thing is to do no harm).

3. The patient should be actively and knowledgeably involved in his own treatment. The relationship between doctor and patient should be one of mutual co-operation, between two specialists, each of whom has specialised knowledge and experience.
This means that there is no longer any place for the authoritarian stance of orthodox medicine, and the view, so often stated, that *Doctor knows best*.

4. Each patient is unique and individual, and must be met and responded to as such. This means that there is no longer any place in medicine for classifying diseases and people. Each disease situation must be looked at as that of an individual in need of help. No two people are precisely the same, and therefore every situation is unique, and requires an individual approach.

APPLIED TO CANCER, THESE CONCEPTS IMPLY THAT THE TUMOUR IS NOT TO BE REGARDED AS THE PRIMARY DISEASE, BUT RATHER AS A MANIFESTATION OF AN UNDERLYING STATE OF IMBALANCE. To date, however, Western medicine insists on

15

regarding the tumour as the primary disease, and in confining its therapeutic efforts to eradicating the tumour. It pays no attention to the underlying state of imbalance, which has resulted in the appearance of the tumour, or to the natural processes of self-healing which exist within the body. Since the underlying state of imbalance is left to continue operating unchecked, it is scarcely surprising that such therapy, while often strikingly successful in eliminating the primary tumour, is generally a good deal less successful when it comes to preventing recurrences at a later date. It is precisely in this area that the need for a new approach is seen to be so necessary. Moreover, the means employed to exterminate the tumour are in the main destructive, relying upon surgery, radiation and cytotoxic chemicals, which are employed with little or no regard to their subsequent effects upon the self-healing power of the body. Thus we see heroic and mutilating operations being performed, such as radical mastectomy, laryngectomy, abdomino-perineal resections, and total hysterectomy etc. without any regard to the well-known fact that surgical shock is damaging to the immune system in itself, while the psychological consequences of the surgery are of even greater significance in the long term prognosis. In addition, massive doses of radiation, cytoxic drugs and steroids are employed with little recognition of their damaging effects upon the immune system, and their disruptive influence upon the body's natural system of tumour defence.

In the personal experience of the writer as a family doctor extending over 35 years, it has seemed that some 75 per cent of the various diseases presented in the consulting room have been of psychosomatic origin. That is to say they are the end products of forces generated within the psyche by the patient, which have arisen in destructive emotional patterns and inadequate mental responses to the varying problems and challenges of life. Their effect is to disrupt the normal functioning of the body, and, through their disturbance of physiological mechanisms, to lead to disease within the body. Of the remaining 25 per cent, most were seen to be the consequence of gross disregard of the normal laws of healthy living, such as eating the wrong foods, living in unhealthy environments, adopting wrong life styles, doing wrong jobs and so on. Genetics, of course, also plays a part in the disease process, but this part is, in the main, limited to determining which target areas within the creature are to break down under the influence of stress.

The term *psychosomatic* is, in this context, not considered to mean functional disease, for which no physical support can be found, but to indicate actual physical changes within the body (soma) brought about by forces arising within the psyche. Any change within the life of a creature/creates a demand upon the body, a response often referred to as stress. If the creature has difficulty in adapting to the change or challenge, the physical response to that challenge may become habitual, and lead, in course of time, to physical breakdown. Although the actual change which is faced by the body, the *stressor*, is often considered to be stress, in the opinion of the writer, stress may more properly be considered to be the state of mind resulting from inadequate adaptation to the stressor, or stress-provoking situation. Change and challenge are to be found throughout life, and are inseparable from life. It is when the response is inadequate that stress results. Moreover, the determining factor in the response is usually how the stress-provoking situation is perceived by the creature; in fact, the meaning of the challenge to the individual. This view implies that the removal of stress, so necessary in the healing of disease, is best dealt with by the *reprogramming* of the mind and of the emotions, rather than by attempts, which are generally impossible anyway, to remove the environmental challenge.

If the antecedents to any breakdown in resistance to common infections — e.g. the common cold, influenza, streptococcal infections and the like — are studied carefully, it will not infrequently be found that the loss of resistance to a common pathogen has been preceded by exposure to a stress-provoking situation which the patient has had difficulty in handling. It is known that such situations provoke changes in hormone secretions within the body, and that these, if prolonged, lead to an increase in steroid production. It is also known that steroids tend to diminish the immune response, and they are, indeed, used clinically for this purpose. This

17

suggests that a prime factor in cancer may well be a breakdown in the immune functioning of the body, and that, in this respect, it is little different from other degenerative diseases. This view is borne out by the oft-repeated observation that a patient, previously living in more or less comfortable symbiosis with his cancer, will break down and lose control of the cancer when confronted with a severe emotional challenge.

It is medical axiom that diagnosis must always precede treatment, and a further axiom that treatment must always be directed primarily towards the cause of the disese, and only after that towards the symptoms of the disease. However, if the diagnosis is to be complete — in the holistic view — such diagnosis must not be limited merely to the identification of the disease, important though that is. If the prime cause is to receive therapy, and that prime cause lies, as it so often does, within the psyche, then the act of diagnosis must attempt to answer not only the question "What is this patient suffering from?", but also the far more difficult and searching question, "Why is **this** patient suffering from **this** disease at **this** moment? Only when this has been done, has the situation been thoroughly thought through, and only then is the therapist in a position to apply therapy at the level of the cause. Judged from this stand-point, modern cancer therapy remains, on the whole, largely empirical, in that it confines its therapy to the tumour, instead of regarding this, as it appears to the writer, as the result of an underlying state of imbalance within the whole person. It is **essential**, if we are ever to make any real headway with the treatment of cancer, that our processes of research be widened so as to give due weight to the emotional, psychological and nutritional factors involved.

The prime physiological factor in cancer seems to lie in the blocking of the control system within the genes, by which a cell undergoes division for the purpose of cell replacement stops dividing, and matures into a fully developed bone, skin, gland, muscle, blood or connective tissue cell. When this happens, such cells, instead of maturing, become arrested in a semi-embryonic state, in which they have no other function than to continue dividing. A blockage of this type may be the result of chemical interference by external *carcinogens*, or viral invasion, and there is evidence to suggest that both of these factors may be involved on occasions. It is thought by a number of people today that there may be from time to time in most bodies cells which *go off the rails* in this way, and fail to develop properly. (One authority has stated that there may be as many as 100,000 such abnormal cells present in healthy people at any one time.) It is certainly a fact that post mortem examinations of people who have died from causes other than cancer not infrequently show collections of cancerous cells, without the patient showing any signs of cancer, and the frequency with which this occurs considerably exceeds the incidence of cancer. It seems, therefore, that in most people there is a mechanism by which the body keeps these abnormal cells in check, and prevents them from developing into a life-threatening disease. The healthy body, of a person who does not develop cancer would seem to treat these cells in the same way as it treats any other foreign cell. That is to say, it recognizes them as being abnormal, and destroys them in the same way as it destroys viruses, bacteria and transplant cells. There *foreign* cells are rejected by the host, and become the prey of the cells of the immune system, particularly the macrophages and the T-lymphocytes. According to this way of thinking, the difference between the cancer patient and the healthy person would seem to lie in the failure of the immune system either to recognise the cells as being abnormal, or to be able to destroy them. This in its turn, according to the holistic view, is probably due partly to the effects of *stress* and partly to dietetic faults resulting in inadequate T-lymphocyte functioning. Evidence in favour of the role of the immune system in this process is provided by the observation that the incidence of cancer in renal transplant patients, where the immune system has been suppressed to reduce the risk of rejection, is 2.5 – 4.1 times that of non-transplant patients. (The variation in the figure is consequent upon the different types of cancer involved, the higher figure being for that including skin cancers.)

Biologically the cancer cell differs profoundly from the normal cell. The normal healthy cell carries a negative charge upon the cell membrane. It obtains the energy necessary to maintain its function by a system of oxidation, and it is recognised by the body system. The cancer cell, on the other hand, carries a positive charge. It is surrounded by a protective coating of psyalomucin, which renders it inaccessible to the immune system cells. It obtains its energy by the anaerobic fermentation of glucose to lactic acid. Its material requirements for growth are met by a protein grab from all over the body, thus leading to a high protein need by the body. Further, the absorption of protein from the diet is hindered by the failure of the replacement of cells in the small intestine, thus leading to a malabsorption of protein. The result is that the body starves to death. These biochemical features of the cancer cell have a profound significance for the therapy of cancer, as will be seen later.

The theory of immune system failure referred to above is known as the *surveillance theory*, and it is beginning to command an increasing measure of support among certain sections of the medical profession. There is a considerable body of evidence in its favour, of which perhaps the most striking is the case outlined below. This was described by Dr Ronald Glasser in his book *The Body is the Hero*. In a rare incident a kidney with undetected cancer nodules was transplanted into a patient. (The donor, of course, had shown no signs of cancer.) The recipient had received the customary preoperative course of immuno-suppressive therapy, and, as usual, this was continued after the operation to prevent rejection of the transplanted kidney. Within days of the operation the transplanted kidney began to enlarge. Initially this looked like some form of rejection, but the transplanted kidney continued to function normally. A few days later a routine X-ray revealed a tumour in the patient's chest. Since a pre-operative X-ray taken four days before going for surgery had been entirely normal, this was clearly something that had arisen since operation. The following day a similar X-ray revealed a tumour in the other lung. When an emergency operation was performed, the transplanted kidney was found to have a mass of cancerous cells at the upper pole amounting to three times its normal size. The physicians came to the conclusion that the deposits in the lungs were metastatic deposits from the primary in the kidney. The interesting thing was the speed with which the deposits had grown, which was far in excess of that normally experienced. There was no choice but to stop administering the immuno-suppressive drugs. Dr Glasser reports:

"Within days, as the patient's immune system came back to normal, the masses in the lungs began to shrink in size. But with the stoppage of the drugs it became obvious that as the patient began to *reject* the cancerous cells, he also began to reject the transplanted kidney. They had no choice. They could not run the risk of the tumour returning, so they kept the patient off the immuno-suppressive drugs. The cancer was destroyed, but the kidney was also rejected. The rejected kidney was removed and the patient put back on chronic dialysis. He survived without further evidence of the cancer."

This important piece of evidence should be known to every oncologist in the land. Its implications for the therapy of cancer are immense. It also supports very strongly the surveillance theory of cancer.

If then the true cause of cancer lies in a breakdown of the immune system, we are left with the questions, "Why does this happen in some people and not in others?" Furthermore, "Why do some cancer patients respond to treatment and recover, while others, who are apparently in an identically similar state as far as their cancer goes, and are receiving identically similar treatment, succumb to their disease?" How DO cancer patients differ from other people, and among themselves?

As has already been mentioned, when the writer started to address himself to the question of WHY people got ill among his own patients, one of the things which struck him most forcefully was the number of times in which a breakdown of resistance to some common infection was the sequel to some emotional challenge or stressful combination of circum-stances which the patient had had difficulty in handling. This was especially plain in young children in whom the emotional patterns were frequently far less complex and more obvious than in adults. Most parents will recall with rueful amusement the number of times when excitements like Christmas, birthday parties, holidays, school examinations and the like were the signal for a loss of immunity to some common pathogen with which the child had coped perfectly well during the preceding months. Amongst adults, too, it is always when we are overstretched in some way, through work, emotional stress or domestic or financial upheaval, that we fall ill. Further weight is given to this by the findings of Holmes and his associates at Washington University Medical School. Holmes tabulated in order of severity and assigned numerical values to the various upheavals that can occur in life. To this scale of numbers he gave the name *The Social Readjustment Scale*. A large sample of volunteers was then investigated over a period of twelve months, with careful assessment of all the incidents in their lives, ranging from traumatic happenings, such as bereavement or divorce down to the trivial, such as a row with the mother-in-law. (It is interesting, too, to note that not all the events were unpleasant. Some were the very opposite, such as promotion at work, marriage and the birth of a child. These, too, can be productive of stress, if not handled in the right way.) At the end of the year the total scores were added up and set against the number of days lost from work through sickness. It was found conclusively that in 75 per cent of people studied morbidity correlated with the score obtained from the *Social Readjustment Scale*.

The concept of *target areas* is frequently spoken of these days, and it appears to the writer that in nearly all individuals there are certain target areas which are prone to breakdown when the individual is subjected to a higher level of change to challenge than he is equipped to handle. Not infrequently these target areas are genetically determined, so that it is common to observe certain diseases, such as diabetes, allergies, cardiovascular disease, asthma and cancer running through successive generations of particular families. But in almost every case there seems to be necessary an emotional or stress factor for the actual development of the disease. An example of this is to be found in the observation that in all patients suffering from rheumatoid arthritis, spondylitis and sacroiliac disease there is present a particular amino-acid, known as LN17, on the genes of the sixth chromosome. However, further research indicated that this was present in no less than 20 per cent of the population, while the total incidence of the diseases in question amount to no more than 2 per cent. It is as if genetics loads the gun, but that to fire it requires a further pressure on the trigger. Could it just be that the cancer patient, too, is one in whom the patterns of surveillance have broken down through the agency of patient-generated stress?

It was remarked in the second century A.D. by Galen that "Melancholic women are more subject to tumours than sanguine women". Gendon, in 1701, drew attention to the importance in cancer of "disasters in life such as occasion much trouble and grief". Burrows, in 1723, stated "Cancer is caused by the uneasy patterns and passions of the mind with which the patient is strongly affected for a long time', which sounds remarkably like an eighteenth century description of stress. Nunn, wrote in *Cancer of the Breast*, in 1802, that: "Emotional factors can influence the growth of cancer". The great Sir James Paget wrote in 1870: "The cases are so frequent in which deep anxiety, deferred hope and disappointment are quickly followed by the growth and increase of cancer that we can hardly doubt that mental depression is a weighty addition to the other influences favouring the cancerous constitution". In 1893 Snow carried out a statistical study of 250 case histories and found that no less than 203 showed stress such as privation and bereavement. He concluded: "Of all causes of the cancer process in every shape, neurotic agencies are the most powerful. Of the most prevalent kinds, distress of mind is that most commonly met with, exhausting toil and privation ranking next. These are direct exciting causes that exert a weighty predisposing influence towards the development of the rest. . . . Idiots and lunatics are remarkably free from cancer in every shape".

Coming nearer to modern times, in 1926 Elida Evans carried out a sophisticated study of 100 cancer patients by Jungian depth psychotherapy. She reported that the typical cancer patient had lost an important emotional relationship before the development of the cancer, and was unable to secure an effective outlet for his or her psychic energy. This view was echoed by Le Shan and Worthington, who wrote: "Cancer patients often showed marked tension over the

23

recent loss of a vital relationship for which there was no available substitute. Such patients had lost the ability to display hostile reactions". In his book *You Can Fight For Your Life: Emotional Factors in the Causation of Cancer*, Le Shan identifies four typical strands in the life histories of the cancer patients with whom he worked. The numbers amounted to over 200 patients, some of whom were counselled in depth over a five year period.

1) The patient's youth was neglected and marked by feelings of isolation and despair, with intense personal relationships appearing difficult and dangerous.

2) In early adulthood the patient was able to establish a strong meaningful relationship, either with a person or role or vocation in life. All his energies were channelled into this relationship, which became the centre of his life and almost his sole reason for living.

3) This relationship or role then became lost, through bereavement, retirement, a move, a child leaving home, or so on. The result was despair, and the reactivation of the childhood sense of loneliness and frustration.

4) One of the funamental characteristics of these people was their inability to express their emotions when they felt hurt, angry or hostile. They were often spoken of as: "She was such a good, sweet person", or as "Such a saint". The benign quality of goodness of these people was, in fact, a sign of their failure to believe in themselves sufficiently, and of their lack of hope.

He then goes on to describe the emotional state of his patients after they had lost the all-important central relationship of these intensely moving words:

"The growing despair that each of these people faced appears to be strongly connected with the loss that each suffered in childhood. They saw the end of the relationship as a disaster they had always half expected. They had been waiting for it to end, waiting for rejection. And, when it came, they said to themselves, "Yes, I knew it was too good to be true?" . . . From a superficial point of view they all managed to adjust to the blow. They continued to function. They went about their daily business. But the colour, the zest, the meaning of life went out of their lives. They no longer seemed attached to life. To those around them, even to people close to them, they seemed to be coping perfectly well . . . But it was the false peace of despair that they felt. They were simply waiting to die. For that seemed the only way out . . . And there they stayed, waiting without hope for death to release them. Within six months to eight years, in my patients, the terminal cancer appeared."

Le Shan reports that 76 per cent of all cancer patients whom he interviewed shared this basic emotional life history. Only 10 per cent of a control group of non-cancer patients showed the same pattern.

These findings have been confirmed by a number of other workers. In this respect, the findings of Dr Caroline Thomas, a psychologist at Johns Hopkins University, Baltimore, are doubly important, in that they are prospective rather than retrospective. (Criticism of Le Shan's findings is frequently raised that the findings could well have been the consequence of the cancer, rather than a predisposing cause, and that, in any case, Le Shan's own beliefs might well have resulted in him influencing the evidence through his own attitudes.) Dr Thomas' important study overcomes these objections. Dr Thomas began interviewing medical students in the 1940s and followed their history of illness over the succeeding years. She was, at that time, less interested in cancer than in the psychological patterns of cardiovascular disease. She reports, from a study of over 1,300 subjects, that the most distinctive psychological profiles belonged to those students who subsequently developed cancer. In particular, her data showed that these students saw themselves as having experienced a lack of closeness with parents, seldom demonstrated strong affections, and that they were generally low key personalities.

During the 1950s Dr David Kissen studied the differences between heavy smokers who developed cancer and those who did not. He found that, among the smokers whom he interviewed, those who developed cancer seemed to have poorly developed facilities for the discharge of emotions of hurt, hostility, resentment or grief. This repression of expression of negative emotions has been found by the writer to be a very common constituent of the personalities.

Drs A. H. Schmale and H. Iker observed in their female cancer patients a particular kind of *giving up*: a sense of hopeless frustration surrounding a conflict to which there was no solution. Often this occurred approximately six months before the development of the cancer. In a further group of persons considered from biological tests to be predisposed towards cancer, using psychological method to identify a *helplessness-prone personality*, they were able to predict 73.6 per cent accuracy which women would subsequently develop cancer.

Dr A. W. Greene studied the psychological and social experiences of patients who developed leukaemia and lymphoma over a period of 15 years (these are forms of cancer). He too observed that the loss of an important relationship was a significant element in the life history of the patient. For both men and women, Greene observed, the greatest loss was the death, or threatened death, of a mother, or in the case of men, a mother figure such as a wife. He concluded that leukaemia or lymphoma occurred in an environmental setting in which the patient had been confronted with a number of losses and separations which had resulted in a state of despair, hopelessness and discontinuity. The writer, too, has found among his own patients that a sequence of losses and personal traumas within a relatively short space of time, is a feature in the history of cancer patients, even among those who do not conform to the life history pattern of Le Shan.

The following case histories, chosen at random from the writer's files, would seem to bear this out.

1) A. was 61. At the age of 60 he underwent compulsory redundancy from his post of senior civil engineer for his County Council. He had never considered the prospect of

retirement nor made any preparation for it, and he resented intensely being *put on the shelf* when he felt he still had so much to contribute from his lifetime of experience. The retirement also involved a considerable drop in his standard of living. Unwisely he sold his house in the pleasant county town in which he had lived so long and bought a small chalet-bungalow in a village some 80 miles away. Here he settled down to try to adapt to his new environment, still seething with discontent over his enforced retirement, and with very little interest or aptitude for the pursuits of village life in an alien community. Within six months of arrival he had developed a carcinoma of the lung, and in a further six months he was dead.

2) E. was 47. She was the child of dominating, non-conformist parents, the second of a large fmaily, brought up during the war in a depressed Welsh mining village. Her father was an alcoholic, out-of-work, Welsh miner. She formed no close relationship with him, and her mother ws always too much engaged with the younger members of the family for any close ties to develop. She felt isolated and lonely as a child, since what time her mother did have to spare was spent in giving aid to others in the village who were in an even worse state. As soon as she left school, she took a job in London as a secretary. Here she met and became engaged to a boy from her own village, of whom her parents disapproved as *not being good enough for her.* She married in the teeth of parental disapproval. Some considerable time later her husband started an affair with a girl from the office. Within six months of this she had developed a carcinoma of the breast.

3) D. is 67. She was brought up in a happy home, the second child of a family of four. Her father died when she was 12. Her mother was a dominating woman of strong personality, and though she was fond of her mother, there was little or no demonstration of affection between the two. When she grew up, she remained at home to look after and help her mother with the younger children. She continued to stay at home until she was 47, when she married. Her mother was angry at the marriage, and bitterly opposed to losing her daughter's care. Three years later her husband

died. She then got work as a secretary and book keeper on a large farming estate. Here she spent 15 happy years. She was good at her work, and developed an affectionate relationship with her employer, becoming almost part of the family. At length the farm estate, which was part of a family trust, became the subject of wrangling between different members of the family. Her employer was forced to give up his interest and move out. One day, she discovered in a farming paper an advertisement for a secretarial post at the estate, and shortly after four applicants arrived at her office. Nothing had been said to her, and when she enquired of the estate agent whether these were for her post, she received no answer to her letter. Her world had crumbled about her, and she felt bitter and resentful both at her own treatment and for that meted out to her employer. She never felt able to express her feelings on the subject. Though she was eventually offered asubstantial sum in compensation for the loss of her post, this did little to mitigate her feelings. Shortly after this she developed a carcinoma of the throat which was inoperable. (It is interesting to note that the throat frequently becomes the seat of trouble in persons unable to express their feelings verbally.) A younger sister had died from a similar condition at the age of 25.

4) F. was an agricultural worker, who lived with his wife and only daughter deep in the depths of the country. When the girl was 14, she became pregnant by a fellow pupil at the local school. He was a wild and unpredictable youth, and there was never any thought of a permanent association. The parents did not believe in taking life which God had given, and so they and their daughter together decided that she would be allowed to have her baby — there were no obstetrical reasons for termination — and that after the birth they would care for the baby while their daughter went back to school to finish her education. When the child was six, the girl became engaged to a young man who was quite prepared to accept the baby as his own. After the marriage the young couple moved away to a distance of about 15 miles. F. had never been able to accept or forgive the seduction of his daughter, nor adequately to express his anger and humiliation over it. He used to lie in bed at night, talking angrily in his sleep about it and grinding his

teeth. However, he became intensely fond of his grandson, and developed a measure of compensation in this. Within six months of the second blow, in which he lost both his daughter and the child he had grown to love, he developed a carcinoma of the lung, and within a further six months he was dead.

5) H. is 47. Seven years previously she underwent a radical mastectomy for breast cancer. Earlier this year she had developed carcinoma in the other breast and underwent another radical mastectomy. There was a family history of cancer, her mother having died from breast cancer when she was four years old. When H. was eight, her father married again. The new wife proved to be an immature, 22 year old girl, who refused to play the role of mother. She refused to be addressed as *Mummy* or to be kissed by the child. She soon became so jealous that she stopped the father going up to kiss the child good-night. After four years of this sort of life the father died of a heart attack. The step-mother refused to care for H., who was sent to an aunt to be brought up. Now aged 12, she was sent to a boarding school, where no interest was taken in her, and she did no work. She left at the age of 16 with no academic qualifications. She was an artistic child, who had always wanted to be a ballet dancer, but she grew too big for this. At the age of 18 she joined the WRNS for the duration of the war. Here, for the first time in her life she was happy. She found in her fellow ratings the companionship which she had always craved, and in the care and interest of her officer a substitute for the maternal care which she had never had. At the end of the war she married a fellow rating, who had gone on to the University, and subsequently went on to a brilliant career in research biology. This resulted in frequent changes of domicile — no fewer than 14 in 30 years of married life. At the age of 30 she had a son, who turned out to be as academically undistinguished as his mother. This was a source of stress to all three. The boy felt himself to be a failure, and the mother felt guilty about this. H.'s second cancer developed following the decision of her husband to take early retirement and move house yet again. Prior to this they had been settled for some years, and H. had developed an interest and expertise in country dancing, thus fulfilling her

need for artistic self-expression and for social contacts. They spent nearly a year looking for an acceptable house into which to move, and when they finally moved, there was no opportunity for H. to resume her dancing. Her second radical mastectomy was then carried out.

6) M. was 47, and the youngest of three children born to Irish parents. A maternal uncle had died of carcinoma of the colon, and before the pregnancy the mother developed leukaemia, for which termination was advised. This was refused owing to their Catholic background. M. was deeply attached to her mother, but feared her father, who was always out drinking with his mates, and frequently came home drunk. When she was eight years old, her mother died of the leukaemia, and that same night her father beat her as having been the cause of her mother's death. Presently the father married again. His new wife was a woman with four children, two of whom were still at school. On the insistence of the step-mother, H. was removed from school and sent out to work so that the step-sisters could remain at school. She had been doing well at school. She took a post as a mother's help, where she lived in and was paid 10 shillings a week to look after the children and run the house. After a year her mistress left the home for employment in Liverpool, saying that M. could run the house better than she could. Finding her position impossible in a small village, H. left to join her sister in London. The two girls found work as chamber-maid and barmaid in a small Kensington hotel. Presently M., now aged 19, started to sing in nightclubs and bars. Subsequently she went abroad to sing in the nightclubs of Athens, Cyprus and, finally, Beirut. Shortly afterwards the Lebanese civil war commenced, and the nightclubs were closed down by the curfew. H. had saved no money to return home, and had no permit to work. She had to live a hand-to-mouth existence, singing in the sleazier bars and hotels, always just one jump ahead of the military police, and never knowing whether she would have enough money to pay for her room and food. She developed a carcinoma of the colon like her uncle, and was admitted to hospital where she underwent surgery. She was finally repatriated, penniless, to Britain by the consulate. A recurrence appeared in the operation scar after return, for

which radiation therapy was given. Shortly after this she married and became pregnant. This was followed by a carcinoma of the bile duct. The pregnancy was terminated and a course of cobalt radiation given which failed to control the disease. She then started to look for an alternative approach.

These examples show graphically and dramatically the points raised in the previous discussion. Especially must there be noted in the final history the damaging effects of childhood deprivation, together with prolonged privations and emotional insecurity in an individual already predisposed towards cancer through a genetic tendency. Also must there be noted the influence of feelings of guilt, unexpressed anger and resentment, and the repression of creative drive. Indeed, in view of what has been said, it would have been remarkable if M. had not developed cancer.

However, one must beware of over-simplicity in our approach. It is likely that cancer occurs when there is a combination of a number of different factors in a susceptible individual. Amongst these are exposure to chemical toxins, radiation, inadequate diet, and exposure, as in a recent example in China, to carcinogenic toxins in the diet. All of these, together with genetics and, possibly, viral infection, can play a part in initiating the cancerous process. All of these have to be taken into account. However, it is necessary to remember that not all exposed to similar hazards, develop the disease. For instance, it is not generally appreciated that while exposure to atomic radiation following the release of atomic bombs over Japan resulted in a vast increase in the incidence of malignant disease, there were a substantial number of people within the area exposed to radiation who did NOT develop such disease. Similarly with other environmental carcinogens, there are many people who do not develop cancer following exposure. There must, therefore, be other factors involved, and, among these, the importance of the psychogenic factor cannot be overemphasised. None of these external factors is a full explanation, without pausing to consider why some individuals, at particular points in their lives, develop cancer. They have certainly been exposed to harmful influences at other times; if there is a genetic predisposition, it has been there all along; their diet is unlikely to have been changed for a number of years. So the question remains to be answered — and our profession, obsessed with years of research for an external cause, seems reluctant to put it — *Why do these particular patients develop cancer at that moment? Why do not all patients similarly exposed?* If, as is postulated by the surveillance theory, abnormal cells occur from time to time in the bodies of all, whether they are created in response to external factors, or whether they occur spontaneously, what lapse in the body's defences allows these cells to develop into a life-threatening tumour at that particular moment? (If, as is being suggested by some, the villain of the piece is an invading virus, one would expect epidemiological studies to reveal some evidence of this, both in location and timing. As this is patently not so, there must be other factors involved which determine the incidence of cancer.) The writer would submit that the balance of probabilities appears to suggest very strongly that these include an interference by stress with the normal immune process of the body, and that very probably these immune processes have been still further weakened by incorrect feeding habits. It is further submitted that our present concept of stress as residing in the surrounding environment is incomplete: that it is not so much the particular stressors which the individual is facing at that particular moment, which are the determining factor, but rather the MEANING of these to him, and how he reacts to them. It is further submitted that the nature of this reaction is very largely determined by the habits and patterns of thought and emotion, which have been laid down over the years, and that the nature of these stems very largely from the early experiences and interpersonal relationships within the family.

The main reason for the continuing blindness of the medical community to this connection lies in its tendency to view the body as a machine, compounded of cells and organs, and contained within the boundaries of its skin. Such a view has blinded the profession to the realisation of the supreme importance of the mind/body relationship as a causative factor in the production of disease. Until the medical profession moves beyond the Cartesian concept of *le Bête*, and recognises that mind and body, together with spirit, constitute a single functioning entity, there is little hope for any real progress in the management of cancer, or any other of the degenerative diseases which now dominate the health scene in the western world. It can be readily seen, within the personal experience of all who read this paper, that even susceptibility to infection is greatly influenced by this relationship. While it is generally recognised that certain diseases, such as peptic ulcer, cardiovascular disease, migraine and asthma, to name but a few, are related to emotional stress, there has so far been a reluctance to accept that many of the degenerative diseases and the hormonal diseases are also intimately concerned in the psychosomatic equation. There is not space to quote all the evidence, but attention is drawn again to the *Social Readjustment Scale* developed by Holmes and his associates. Using these objective measurements, Holmes was able to predict patterns of illness in his subjects with a high degree of accuracy. No fewer than 49 per cent of the high scoring subjects developed illness over the 12 months of the study, as compared with only 9 per cent of the low scoring subjects, over the same period. However, even this method of predicting illness falls short of absolute accuracy. The missing factor, not accounted for in the tables, would appear to be that while it is possible to predict the *probability* of illness as a consequence of stressful circumstances, it is not possible to predict how the individual will REACT to the stressful situation, and that it is this REACTION — the MEANING OF THE SITUATION TO THE PERSON — which is the crucial factor in determining both the development of disease and the nature of the disease which develops.

Part of the problem of the slowness of the medical community to acknowledge the role of stress in disease has been due to the difficulties inherent in understanding the actual neuro-physiological mechanism by which emotional states and habit patterns affect body physiology, and thus contribute to the onset of illness. Without such an understanding, the concept is dismissed as fantasy. In recent years, however, research into the effects upon physiology of chronic stress has begun to delineate such a mechanism. Again, space does not permit going through the evidence, but attention is drawn to the work of Hans Selye (*The Stress of Life*, McGraw-Hill, New York: 1956. *Stress without Distress*, Lippincott, Philadelphia: 1974), and to the work of Greer and his colleagues at King's College Hospital. Greer observed that raised blood levels of serum IgA were found in women who habitually suppressed emotions of anger and hostility, and that the survival time in breast cancer was lessened in those in whom such levels were raised. Suppression of these emotions was found to be a characteristic of the personalities of many women with breast cancer. In summary, it might be said that stress, which consists of chronic stimulation of the *fight-flight-fright* response, without adequate framework for its discharge through physical activity, has the following effects:

1) It frequently produces hormonal disturbances and imbalances. Since hormones play a crucial role in regulating body functions, these can eventually lead to over- or under-stimulation of the sympathetic-parasympathetic system. Hypertension, atheroma and subsequent renal failure are examples of this process in action.

2) It depresses the immune system responsible for attacking and destroying abnormal cells. As has been already pointed out, such abnormal cells may be the result of invasion from without — as in the case of infections — or may have originated within the body during the process of cellular replacement. It may also be the case that certain external invaders interfere with cell biochemistry by blocking essential control mechanisms, thus resulting in the production of abnormal cells.

3) In view of our current ignorance about the mechanisms responsible for the control of cellular growth and replacement, it may well be that these imbalances actually increase the tendency for the production of abnormal cells at precisely the moment when the body is least capable of destroying them. The findings of Greet *et al.* with reference to serum IgA may well fit into this area.

If the contention that a major prime factor in cancer is to be found in the failure of the immune system to protect the patient against the uncontrolled proliferation of abnormal cells, and that such failure is closely related to, if indeed not the actual consequence of, influences arising within the psyche, it is to the correction of these influences, and to the re-establishment of the immune system that the main thrust of cancer therapy needs to be directed. Any system of therapy, which ignores this and concentrates its efforts upon destroying the tumour, rather than neutralising the forces encouraging its growth, seems, to this observer at least, to be avoiding the main issue. Such a system could be likened to prescribing codeine for the aching tooth instead of advising a visit to the dentist. Though highly effective in the short run, such a procedure is fraught with the inevitable return of the pain as soon as the effect of the codeine wear off. It is in this area that the present methods of cancer seem to be the most deficient.

Immune-system deficiency may be broken down into two main areas: firstly, as has been already described, that arising from psychological causes; secondly, dietary factors influencing T-cell production. It is proposed to consider first the dietary factors, and leave the other area to a later chapter.

All the naturopathic systems of therapy in use today in cancer treatment lay great stress upon correct eating habits. These include the well-known and generally undervalued regimes of Gersson and Kelly in America, Moerman in Holland, Issls in Germany, and Forbes in the United Kingdom. Some of these claim high rates of success in patients given up by orthodox medicine. To understand the possible reasons for this is it necessary to look at the working of the immune system. This seems to be largely dependent upon the correct functioning of the T-cells. Zurier, at the University of Connecticut, showed that animals with systemic lupus and arthritis, in which T-lymphocyte function was defective, can be treated successfully with injections of Prostaglandin E1, which stimulates the T-lymphocytes and controls the disease. Bailey, at George Washington University, showed that most cancer cell lines and virus transformed cells lack a critical enzyme which would enable them to make

Prostaglandin E1. A deficiency here could be a vital reason behind the failure of the immune system in cancer. There would appear to be a case for administering vitamin C in megadoses together with small quantities of zinc in all cases of cancer, and for ensuring that adequate supplies of the unsaturated fatty acid, linoleic acid, which is available only from certain vegetables (notably plants of the borage family), are available in the diet. (For a more detailed consideration of T-cells and Prostaglandin E1, see the technical notes in Appendix B.) This should be combined with restrictions upon carbohydrate consumption, dairy products, meat protein and opium-containing drugs or their derivatives. Curiously enough, T-cell production seems to be stimulated by small amounts of alcohol (up to a blood level of 18 per cent). This may well be the reason behind the traditional remedy of hot whisky and lemon as the treatment for a cold.

Another of the problems with cancer is the inability of the T-cells to recognise the cancer cells, consequent upon their psyalomucin coating and positive electrical membrane potential. Disintegration or *de-shielding* can be achieved through the administration of beta-carotene and bromelain (an extract of pineapple enzymes). The carotene is best given in the form of carrot juice, always mixed with a little cream or butter to aid absoprtion. Patients with active cancers require to be drinking six to eight classes of carrot juice daily — up to a point where there is a slight yellow staining of the hands. Needless to say, the carrots should come from an organically cultivated source.

Let us recapitulate what we have been saying. The basis of the holistic approach to healing is the recognition of four cardinal principles:

1) Man is a creature of a number of different levels, all of which interact and inter-relate together. Health results when all of these are in a state of balance and harmony. Disease is the end product, at the physical level, of imbalance among these deeper levels. Moreover, since each individual is in a state of interaction and interrelationship with others around him, there has to be harmony and balance between the creature and his environment as well.

2) Each individual contains within him or herself an innate power of self-healing, which operates to restore the balance once a disturbing force has been neutralised or removed. This force, the *Vis Mediactrix Naturae* of the ancients, is the expression of the divine life force within each creature. It is recognised by science as being the homoeostatic tendency, (Gr: *homos*, the same, and *statos*, position) which is a part of all living creatures. It operates in man through the immune system. Thus the healing of disease results from the restoration of balance both within the creature itself, and between the creature and its surroundings, and not from the imposition of change from without.

3) Each patient must be knowledgeably and actively involved in his or her own treatment. The doctor-patient relationship has to be one of mutual co-operation between specialists of equal standing. This means the abandonment of the authoritarian stance *Doctor knows best. It is not necessary for you to know.*

4) Each person is a unique — and precious — individual. Each has had his or her own experiences and traumas in life, which have made him what he-she is and which play a part in determining his response to therapy. It is therefore not possible to categorise and classify patients according to disease structure, since the consequences of whatever therapy is introduced will vary from patient to patient. This means that it is necessary to get away from the practice of looking at the tumour in isolation, and to start looking at the individual who has the tumour.

The application of these principles to the management of cancer is the complete apotheosis of the holistic approach to healing. Cancer is a disease of the total person, and every approach has to be total — i.e. operating on all levels. Further, since each person is a unique individual, so is each case of cancer. Moreover, every case of cancer involves not just the individual, but the family as well. It is a family situation, and needs to be met and responded to as such.

37

Cancer is not something which has attacked the patient from outside (thought environmental consideration may play a part), but something which has been permitted to happen through faulty mental attitudes and emotional relationships, and through errors in life style. For any healing to take place there has to be a reversal of whatever conditions and states of mind have been operating prior to the development of cancer. This can only be achieved through the active and voluntary participation of the patient. Some of the methods in which this may be achieved are discussed in the succeeding chapter.

CHAPTER 2

Meditation and Counselling

Important though the dietetic and biochemical approach is to the therapy of cancer, its effects can be greatly enhanced if due attention is paid to the psyche. Negative attitudes and doomladen expectations are fatal to a successful outcome. The writer has been addressing himself to this aspect of the problem for a number of years, working with cancer patients, both individually, and collectively in a group setting, in attempting to reorientate their attitudes, both to life in general, and to their cancer in particular. The methods employed are psychotherapy and counselling, deep relaxation and meditation combined with visual imagery. With this is given a whole-food diet, in which the main emphasis is upon raw fruit and vegetables and vitamin/mineral supplements. (See appendices for details.) It is proposed to describe the process in detail.

First a detailed psychological history is taken, extending back to earliest childhood. Particular attention is paid to the interpersonal and family relationships, and to any childish reaction to deep emotional trauma which may have occurred during this period. During the taking of this history a full explanation is given of the nature of the cancerous process, and of the role played by the immune system in controlling both the occurrence of infections and the destruction of cancerous cells. The detailed facets of the cancer personality, as described by Le Shan, are set before the patient. Examples are given from other case histories, and it is explained that emotional and psychological factors can and do operate to interfere with the normal process of self-protection. Not infrequently the patient will interrupt at this point with the words: "But, Doctor! You have just described me! I can see myself in what you said." Patients are given the opportunity to discuss their problems, and to try to see within their own lives the processes operating which have affected other people. Every effort is made to get to know the patient as an individual person at the deepest level. "Cancer is what you are doing to yourself through your mind and your emotions", they are told. "If you want to be well, you must first learn to stop doing this to yourself. It is not something which has just happened to you. Your body can heal itself, if you will work towards this end and allow it to do so."

The next task is to remove the sense of hopeless fear which is so apt to engulf the patient once the diagnosis of cancer has been made. Cancer is an emotive word, synonymous for many with a painful and degrading death. The general ethos of the health service, with its emphasis upon permissive acceptance of external intervention, without personal responsibility or involvement in the process, only serves to reinforce the cancer image of hopelessness and rejection. Many people refuse to recognise that they have got cancer, and will employ all sorts of euphemisms to hide the truth from themselves and others. Others react with anger and aggression, which is sometimes extended even to the doctor who has made the diagnosis. Such an attitude however, is infinitely preferable to a stoical attitude of acceptance without involvement, which is characteristic of so many, or to the attitude of hopeless resignation to the inevitable. This latter is comparable to that of the victim of Voodoo, in which his own beliefs and those of his family and friends and neighbours are powerful contributory factors towards a death which is seen by all as inevitable, and met in a state of total emotional and social isolation. Such attitudes are highly destructive, so that complete reorientation of the mind is essential if patients are to stand any chance of survival. Negative attitudes among medical and nursing staff in hospital clinics are powerfully invasive, even if unexpressed outwardly, and, as in the Voodoo death, increase the feeling of hopeless isolation in the patient. Accordingly patients are told that one in 100,000 cancers regress spontaneously, even without therapy, and that of the remainder, from a third to a half are cured by normal therapy, depending upon the nature of the cancer and when they report for therapy. THE BODY HAS ITS OWN SYSTEM OF SELF-DEFENCE, WHICH MUST BE ENCOURAGED AND ALLOWED TO OPERATE. THE DIFFERENCE BETWEEN THEMSELVES AND OTHER PEOPLE WHO HAVE NOT GOT CANCER LIES IN THE FACT THAT THEY ARE PREVENTING THIS FROM HAPPENING. It is necessary for them to be totally involved in their own healing, to be willing to work for it themselves, and not to wait for it to be done for them by someone else. However, there can be little doubt that in about one fifth of the patients with cancer, the cancer represents an unconscious death wish; a desire to escape from a life situation which the patient no longer finds tolerable. With such as these, nothing can be done until they are prepared to face up to the responsibilities of life, and accept the difficulties and the challenges. The motivation for becoming well again MUST come from the patient, and patients are told in clear and unequivocal terms that this is not something which can be done for them by a therapist. While actual physical healing, of course, is never promised, patients are always told that if they will truly co-operate in the programme suggested, and follow the instructions in all their details, then it can be guaranteed that they will feel better, and that, so long as life persists, nothing is impossible if the faith and the will to survive are strong enough. The consultation is concluded with detailed instructions as to diet (a diet sheet and therapy summary are given), use of tobacco, alcohol, and drugs and so on.

Subsequent to this the patient comes back at regular intervals for psychotherapy and counselling, and to share in a meditation session with the therapist. In these follow-up visits patient and therapist work together towards the neutralisation of past negative emotions and their recognition as playing a powerful contributory role in the loss of immune control. Once a patient is able to recognise WHY he or she has got cancer, then a start can be made in helping them to overcome the cancer. Thus patients are asked to consider the changes which have occurred in their lives in the two or three years prior to the development of the cancer, to reflect upon how they met these changes, and whether there were emotional stresses associated with them. If there were, then they must ask themselves whether they are still holding on to these reactions, and must realise that to continue to respond to past traumas with attitudes of bitterness, guilt, or self-pity is a useless waste of energy, and inhibitory to the self-healing process. Patients are taught to value themselves, and that their own needs, both psychological and practical, are at least as important as those of others, if their health is to be maintained. Generally speaking patients with cancer tend to neglect these, and always to play a subservient role in their relationships with others. For many, this is the most difficult task of all. Old habits die hard, and deeply engrained behavioural patterns require constant effort and great determination if they are to be changed. One way in which this is attempted is to require the patient to identify the secondary gains and compensations of their illness. For many the fact of illness can provide important psychological advantages. It can serve as a means of manipulating the behaviour of those around them, or as a way of escape from unwanted responsibilities, or an intolerable work load. Unless these are seen by the patient as important psychological requirements in life, **which have to be satisfied, if health is to be maintained**, but that there are other and better ways of achieving these ends than having cancer, there remains a built-in psychological motive against recovery. Patients and therapist then must work together so as to determine how their life can be reorientated so as to ensure that these needs are met. Patients also have to be taught to look forward rather than backwards, and that the all-important factor in determining the outcome is their own expectation of what that outcome will be. If their personal image of cancer is one of an inevitable downwards progress towards death, then that becomes a powerful instruction to the body to move in that direction. If, on the other hand, their expectation is one of victory and ultimate health, then that constitutes a very effective reinforcement of the body's self-healing power. Thus confidence becomes all important, and every effort has to be made to strengthen the confidence of the patients both in themselves and in their therapy. One way in which this is done is by inviting the patient to select certain goals of achievement or targets in life, which they would like to meet. It is important that these should be both practical, and under the patient's own efforts. These may be as down to earth and mundane as getting a rise at work, reducing their golf handicap, starting a project in the house or going on a desirable holiday. In their meditation and visualisation practice (to be described later) they are then told to visualise the goal as having been ALREADY ACHIEVED, and then, subsequent to the meditation, to break down the achievement of the goal to its various steps. They must then go out and take the first steps necessary to achieve the goal. In meditative terms, this amounts to an act of affirmation, a statement that they EXPECT to live to achieve the goal. (One must realise at this point that the true meaning of the word *expect*, which has been rather lost sight of in modern times, is *await*. The suggestion of a *pious hope* is utterly foreign to the true meaning of the word.) By such means the patient's attitude towards his disease, and the eventual outcome of therapy, becomes subtly reorientated in a positive direction.

The primary tool used is meditation and visual imagery. Patients are taught a simple technique of deep relaxation, and asked to visualise the healing process at work in the body, and instructed to carry this out for 15 minutes three times every day. The crucial importance of regularity is stressed, and they are told, quite bluntly, that if they are not prepared to give this 45 minutes a day to the process of making themselves well, life cannot be a thing which they value very highly, and that they are wasting the writer's time and their own. It is not much of a price to pay when the alternative is death. Whenever possible an effort is made to involve the spouse in the healing meditation. At one time the writer made use of a simple instrument of bio-feedback to monitor the degree of relaxation obtained, and this is still used in some clinics. The writer's experience suggests, that this is not always helpful, since patients may be paying more attention to the instrument than to the process of relaxing. Such an instrument depends, like the *lie-detector*, upon the fact that electrical skin resistance varies with degrees of relaxation and arousal, and that by measuring skin resistance, extremely accurate monitoring of the state of arousal is possible. There are a number of these relaxation meters on the market. That used by the writer for a period is the *Omega 1. E.S.R. Meter*, manufactured by Audios Ltd. of London, but there are others which are equally suitable. (The effects of levels of arousal upon skin resistance was first demonstrated to the British Council in 1905 by Jung and Pederson, but it is only recently that tests have shown how accurately changes in the skin resistance can be correlated with states of arousal and relaxation. An increase of 30 – 40 per cent has been shown to indicate a slow alpha brain rhythm.)

The importance of the depth of relaxation reached rests upon the fact that the more deeply relaxed the body becomes, the more open it is to the suggestive influence of the mind. Thus when, in deep relaxation, and slow alpha rhythm, the patient visualises the assault upon the cancer by white cells of the body's defence system, the body is amenable to this suggestion, and this is what actually happens. In the same way, it is possible, with the aid of biofeedback instruments, to train a person to vary the skin temperature of one hand as compared with the other by several degrees, through the simple expedient of visualising, while in a state of deep relaxation, the hand immersed in a bucket of very hot or very cold water. The cutaneous blood vessels respond to the mental suggestion and behave as if what was being visualised was actually taking place, thus raising or lowering the skin temperature through the variation in the circulation. In a precisely similar way the trained yogi is able to staunch the flow of blood from a wound purely by processes of auto-suggestion.

Whenever possible, patients are brought together every two weeks for a group meditation experience. The importance of this is that a group dynamic is introduced into the situation. Since all patients are facing the same problem of cancer, they no longer feel isolated, and newcomers to the group are able to benefit from the experience of others, and to see just how much they can be helped and how attitudes can change. In the group they are first taken into a state of deep relaxation, with emphasis on quiet rythmical breathing, muscular relaxation, emotional calming and centring of the mind upon the peace of the present moment. During this phase the E.S.R. meter may be used to monitor the depth of relaxation obtained. Following this they are then given a guided meditation of a visual nature into peace, tranquillity and light. Where E.S.R. meters are being used, an increase of about 30 per cent in skin resistance is looked for. (This meditation also serves as a guide for their own meditations at home. Cassettes instructing patients in the steps of meditation are also available, but patients are told that these should only be used during the learning process, and that it is important that they actually do the meditations for themselves, and not just listen to the cassette instead.) Following the guided meditation they are then instructed to turn their centre of consciousness within, and to take a trip through their own bodies, and to try to visualise the area of their disease, and their body's attack upon it. Though this can be done in any imagery which comes to the patient, (the imagery involved is often intensely revealing of the patient's inner attitude towards the disease), they are warned that the cancer should not be seen as something hard and menacing but as a collection of unhappy cells that have lost their way and forgotten their identity; a rather grey and amorphous shape which the body is attacking and destroying through the action of the white cells in the blood. They are told to concentrate upon seeing it gradually getting smaller until it finally disappears altogether. This attack by the body, they are told is under THEIR control, and the intensity and vividness of their visualisation of the attack upon the tumour controls the actual physical level of the response. The imagery at this point requires to be spontaneous, and it is helpful to ask the patient to draw what has been visualised. (Many patients have difficulties with visualisation, and the act of drawing helps to focus and clarify the mental image.) At the conclusion of the visualisation the group are returned to the meditative state of calm peace. The use of music as an aid to relaxation is often helpful. Where this is done, the music requires to be of a faint aetherial nature, without any strong rhythmical or melodic patterns. Harp and flute music is especially valuable in this respect, and a very suitable piece is James Galway's *Song of the Seashore* (Cassette: RCA ARK1 – 3534).

In the writer's practice, patients are given healing at this stage through the hands of a healer. To most orthodox physicians such a process will smack of quackery and mumbo-jumbo, and, indeed, since the whole process is so little understood and runs so counter to the conventional model, so it seems. There is, however, an increasing body of evidence of a concrete nature to suggest that biological activity can be influenced by such methods, possibly through the emanation of some form of energy through the hand of the healer. Indeed, confidential research in this area is at present being carried out by some highly respected and reputable physicians and scientists in some extremely prestigious hospitals. In this respect the classical experimental work carried out by Professor Justa Smith, of the Department of Enzymology at Rosary Hill College, New York, Dr Benard Grad of McGill University, Montreal and Drs Reinhardt and Miller of Anges Scott College, Atlanta, all suggest that much of what has previously been dismissed as fantasy is solidly based on fact, although the explanation at present lies beyond science. If such things do happen, and in the opinion of the writer, the balance of the evidence suggests that they probably do, it seems likely that the healing takes place through the stimulation of the normal process of self-healing and repair, which are inherent in all living creatures. Attention is drawn to the observation of Dr Alexis Currel, recorded in *Man the Unknown*, of the extremely rapid acceleration of the normal process of regression undergone by skin cancer observed under the lens following receiving healing through the hands of a healer.

The writer's group meets every two weeks. Ideally such a group should meet weekly, but in view of the distance that some patients travel to attend the group, this is all that is practicable at the present stage. In any such group there are four key roles to be filled, though it may be possible for more than one role to be filled by the same person. Firstly it is important that a doctor should be seen to be involved. Even if he is unable to attend every meeting he should be present as often as possible. His task is to monitor the results being achieved, to advise and re-assure the patients upon any medical problem that may arise, to act as a bridge between the group and the orthodox wing of the profession, and to create in the mind of the patient the all important aspect of confidence and normality. He also helps to give the group an air of medical respectibility!

The second role is that of group leader. His or her task is to act as a focal point for the group, and to lead the meditations and relaxation of the group. He or she should be one who is already experienced in leading meditation and to working with groups. The third role is that of the psychotherapist. His or her task is to assist in the pyschological evaluation of the patient, and to aid in the all important task of reorientation. Although much of this work will be done on a one-to-one basis through extended sessions of counselling and psychotherapy, the presence at the group of the psychotherapist is also of importance. In many groups the psychotherapist may, because of training and experience, serve as the group leader. Fourthly, though not all will agree with this, the writer suggests that the presence of proven and experienced healers is of the utmost value. It is important that these should be able to be assimilated into the group.

In the opinion of the writer, groups of this nature should be a routine part of every oncology clinic in the land. Although there are already a few such in existence, they are, for the most part, organised by dedicated amateurs, and have not the benefit of medical co-operation. (A noted exception to this is that run at New Haven, Connecticut, by the distinguished surgeon and teacher, Dr Bernard Siegel, of Yale University.) When tackled on this subject, the oncologists have two replies. One is that funding and premises are inadequate for such an approach. The second is that such methods are unproven, and that they cannot be seen to associate themselves with unproven methods, and that, in any case, they are liable to raise false hopes in the patient. This latter point, of course, is nonsense. Doctors are constantly trying out new methods and new approaches. A constant stream of new drugs is coming on to the market, all of which are being researched in hospital clinics. There is NO ethical reason why a trial should not be made of these new ways of managing cancer. Further, in view of the KNOWN IMPORTANCE of the placebo effect in the healing process,

ANYTHING which serves to raise the patient's expectations MUST be a plus factor and on the credit side. It can NEVER be wrong to give hope where no hope exists, and the existence of such hope may well be the one thing which makes the difference between life and death for the patient.

One can, of course, sympathise with and understand such answers. However, when one considers the vast amounts of money raised and disbursed each year on *cancer research*, and contrasts this with the meagre dividends in terms of survival expectations resulting from this expenditure, one is tempted to recall the saying that *'Where there's a will, there's a way'*, and to reflect that establishment attitudes are primarily concerned that it should be THEIR way. Were one tenth of the resources, skill and energy expended on *orthodox* research to be devoted to a systematic examination of the holistic approach, and were these approaches to be applied from the outset, instead of, as mostly happens at present, as a last ditch resort, when all else has failed and the immune system has deteriorated so far under the secondary effects of radiation and chemotherapy as to be incapable of responding, what might not be the results? It seems that there is an overwhelming case for a change of heart among the powers that be, and that a willingness to abandon what has become an entrenched position is what is really needed.

What are the results to be expected from such an approach? It is important here that this be seen in its true perspective as just one part of the holistic approach, and that the psychotherapeutic approach is not taken in isolation from nutrition and metabolic therapy, and healing. Nor does it constitute an ALTERNATIVE to conventional methods. ALL are valid at their own level, and the truly important thing is that this should be combined with conventional therapy. Surgery, radiation and even chemotherapy all have their part to play — at their own level. Provided care is taken to keep in mind at all times the over-riding importance of the immune system in the healing process, they are not out of place. The difficulties in assessment of the new approach arise from the fact that in most cases this is not embarked upon until all conventional methods have been exhausted. By this time the immune response may have been so damaged by orthodox therapies that there is little left with which the patient can fight the disease. These methods need to be employed from the very outset of the disease in combination with discreet use of conventional methods. Unfortunately their existence is frequently regarded by oncologists as a threat to their own position and met with attitudes of hostility and non-cooperation.

Results in any form of cancer therapy are always difficult to assess owing to the long-term nature of the disease. Moreover, in this approach we are dealing with another variable and unpredictable factor, which is not under our control as therapists — the outlook and attitude of the patient. Furthermore, some of the effects of such an approach do not readily lend themselves to quantification. Wellness and health are largely subjective experiences, and cannot be measured. Scientifically speaking, they exist in a different realm to illness, and obey different laws. However, in the experience of the writer, where embarked upon from the outset, there would appear to be an enhanced response to surgery, and orthodox therapy, such as radiation therapy. Side effects seem to be lessened and to be tolerated more readily. Generally it is found that there is a reduction in the level of symptoms, such as pain, loss of appetite, lethargy, weight loss and depression, and a correspondingly reduced dependence upon analgesics. Almost invariably there is a massive change in the outlook of the patient. (Where this does not occur, it is usually an indication that either the patient does not really wish to recover, or that psychotherapy had failed to reach the inner cause of the cancer.) This is characterised by the acceptance of cancer as just another disease, loss of fear, both of the disease itself, and of dying, and a very real appreciation of the worth of every minute of every day. Life becomes no longer something to be dreaded, or the day to be *got through*, but to be enjoyed. Where, as is always advised, the spouse or consort becomes a supporting member of the group and joins in the meditations, there is a profound healing influence upon the whole family, together with a breaking down of the barriers to communication which are so often erected after cancer has been diagnosed. This is of the utmost importance to the progress of the patient. Finally, in those patients who do not recover, the writer has noticed there is easier and less distressful dying, through the removal of the fear of death, and thus of the desire to cling on to life, however imperfect, until the last possible moment. Such patients are often active and about their daily pursuits until within 36 – 48 hours of death. The writer has described this as *the oiling of the hinges of the door between this world and the next.* The letters of thanks received by the writer from the relatives of patients, who have made the great transition to the wider horizons of the world beyond, are eloquent testimony to this aspect of the therapy.

Ultimately the result will depend upon the stage in which the patients first come for help, the intensity of commitment on the part of the patient, the genetic make-up of the patient, and the degree of intensity of the orthodox, tissue-destroying therapies to which the patient has already been subjected. All too frequently the patient presents in the terminal stages, when the immune system has been so battered by radiation and cytotoxic chemotherapy, that there are few white cells left with which to fight. When patients DO present before surgery, quite remarkable powers of recovery have been noted. Such patients are invariably the *star patients* in their wards, and their post-operative convalescence is conspicuous for its freedom from pain and for the rapidity of healing. For patients who present in the later stages there has been noted, in addition to the effects described above, an apparent prolongation of the expected duration of life, though in cancer this is notoriously difficult to assess, together with an improved quality of life. This alone would appear to be more than adequate justification for the wider adoption of this approach.

As has already been emphasised, it is important that this approach should not be used on its own. Of all diseases cancer most requires a truly holistic approach, in which therapy is extended to the total man at all his levels of being. The body requires therapy as well as the mind and the spirit. There is still a most important role for orthodox therapy, and diet, too, must play an integral and co-ordinating part in the therapeutic approach. The aim of the process is to intensify and reinforce the natural healing powers of the body — the

Vis Medicatrix Naturae — rather than to impose upon the body healing from without. AT ALL COSTS one must seek to avoid damage to these. Thus while there is an important role for surgery, this should often be less radical than it now is. (It must always be remembered that not only is surgical shock damaging to the white cell count, but that the psychological trauma resulting from massive and mutilating operations still further depresses the immune system through reinforcing the negative forces at work within the psyche.) If the primary growth can be removed, it obviously leaves less work for the immune system to do, so that protection against wandering metastases is more easily obtained. Thus, to particularise for a moment, it is to be hoped that lumpectomy will take the place of total and radical mastectomy, and that follow-up procedures will take due note of the potentially damaging effects of radiation upon the immune system.

These potentially damaging effects can be offset to a large degree if radiation is seen as the **ally** rather than the **enemy** of the body in its fight against the cancer. During meditation, both while the radiation is taking place, and afterwards, it should be visualised as a hail of silver bullets striking the cancer cells, but bouncing harmlessly off the healthy cells. In the short term, radiation is a valuable tool against certain cancers, and can often be extremely effective in **buying time** to allow the immune system to recover. Especially is this so in the case of certain bone and brain tumours. It is only when it is indiscriminatingly applied, or applied to excess, that is effects are damaging.

The intent throughout should be to strengthen rather than weaken the immune system. **Above all else, the ancient maxim: *Primum est non nocere*** (the first thing is to do no harm) **should be constantly borne in mind.**

CHAPTER 3

Working with the Holistic Approach

At this point we have to pause for a moment to consider just what it is that we mean by the term "Holistic Approach". To so many people today this implies some sort of alternative road which they can follow to the exclusion of the orthodox forms of medical treatment. To yet others it means any form of therapy which is not practised by "proper doctors" and ranges all the way from comparatively "respectable" therapies like acupuncture and osteopathy, to such bizarre approaches to healing as aromatherapy and gem therapy. (Not that I am making a judgement on these therapies. I simply have not had sufficient experience of them for that. In any case I have seen too many examples of unconventional and, by "scientific" standards inexplicable healings to rule out anything. We simply do not know enough at this stage to form judgements). By Holistic Treatment I mean help given to the Whole Man — at all his levels — and point out that the Holistic Approach is an all embracing package, which has to be applied in its entirety at all those levels. Let the reader who remains in any doubt refresh his memory by re-reading the opening paragraphs of the opening chapter of this book.

What then are the results to be expected from working with this "Holistic Approach"? What advantages can we see over the conventional forms of therapy? In attempting to answer this question we must first understand that this method does not in any way attempt to supplant orthodox therapies. It is not an alternative, although there are those who would seek to make it seem so. It is an extension of care into those areas which are not currently reached by orthodox medicine, and needs to employed in conjunction with orthodox therapies. Moreover, if its full benefits are to be obtained, it is necessary that it be employed from the very outset. Too often those who come to seek this form of help do so when they have exhausted all that orthodox therapy can give; when they have been told, "I am sorry. There is no more that we can do for you. You have had all the radiation or chemotherapy that your body can stand. You must go home and try to make the most of the time remaining to you."

As will have been appreciated by those who have followed the argument this far, the Holistic Approach depends upon the capacity of the body to heal itself and to re-establish control over the errant cancer cells within it. If the patient has been subjected to intense and destructive therapies, it is highly likely that this self-healing power has been so damaged as to be unable to function. In such cases the body has already passed the point of no return and "cure" becomes an impossibility. However, even here, though this is not its prime role, the Holistic Approach remains of value. The objectives of cancer care have been stated by one well-known specialist as being three in number, and in this order of priority: 1. Quality of life. 2. Quality of death. 3. Duration of life. Many cancer patients might disagree with this and put duration of life first in their order of priorities. A moment's pause for reflection, however, will reveal to them that a life dragged on in ever-increasing pain, weakness and physical degradation is something from which they are likely to seek release, rather than prolongation. In such instances the Holistic Approach, even when it is unable to ensure the complete reversal of the cancer, restores a quality in joyful living which far exceeds mere numerical duration of life. The following very beautiful letter from a patient of mine, admittedly one who came before the point of no return had been passed, but who was seriously ill with metastases from a breast cancer following deep personal trauma in life, exemplifies what is meant by "quality of life".

". . . My life is a constant source of mystery as well as joy. Mysterious because, like anyone else, I do not know what the future will bring. Yet prior to having cancer, the thoughts of the future were peripheral ones. The future was something that would always be there. Now I know better. That is where the joy comes in. With each new sunrise there is a beautiful day ahead. A day full of excitement and "hum-drums" too. Nonetheless, it is there for the picking — ripe and full of promise. I like to make my days count. Here is how I have been living.

"Three to four mornings weekly, I exercise in my gym. Sounds grand, but "my gym" is nothing more than an empty room with one mirrored wall, some assorted weights and a rowing machine. My friend, who is an amateur athlete, has designed a two-hour programme which consists of running two miles; lifting weights (for tone and endurance, not muscle bulk); aerobics and dancing. I just love every minute! It is a definite high!

"The other two days you would find me teaching weaving at my daughter, Jennifer's, school. It is a volunteer position. With my background as a primary school teacher, it is a job that I truly enjoy. I built frame looms, one for each child in Jennifer's class. I will travel with the looms, from grade to grade; teaching fine motor skills, math sets, patterns, the history of fabric etc. Next I will do a learning module on honey-bees, from the flower all the way to the honeycombs, the production of honey, worker bees, etc. Volunteer teaching is an excellent tool for me to continue a task I adore, without the daily commitment. Much like the grandparent who can leave when the grandchild becomes a nuisance; still in touch with parenting, but at a comfortable distance.

"Jennifer is also a joy. It is often difficult for parents, as much as for children, to separate. Volumes have been written! Relationships are fascinating, aren't they? At five, Jennifer is a bright, curious, perceptive and sensitive person. We learn a great deal from each other. "My evenings are active, too. I am in charge of fund-raising for my Cancer Research Unit. In addition I started a study group for ten couples to pursue Judaic studies. During the summer I raised money for the International Child Abuse Conference that was here in Montreal (first time in North America.)

"Healthwise, everything is great and shall remain so.

"It is awkward and perhaps impertinent to ask you personal questions as I don't know you on that level. That is why my letter sounds so one-sided. Truthfully I think of you often; as someone who has inspired me with your compassion and your brilliance — both technically and spiritually. Do keep up your work. It is so essential for all of us! When the 'going gets tough', think of me as someone whose life you touched and turned around."

I have quoted this letter from this young and radiant girl because it exemplifies so perfectly what is meant by true healing. So often we tend to confuse curing and healing. But the two are not the same. Cure takes place on the physical level only, and if the condition from which we are suffering originates, as it so often does, from a state of inner disharmony, then this inner force is left still operating. In such a situation relapse, or the development of a further disease process, is almost inevitable. When the inner cause is healed, and the sick person brought into tune with themselves, their fellows, and all around them, then it does not seem to matter so much whether there is healing at the physical level. In many cases there will be — provided that the self-healing power of the body has not been too far damaged. But sometimes there will not be physical healing in the full sense of the word, as the following case history shows.

J. was a woman of sixty-seven when she first came to see me. She was suffering from a malignant ovarian cyst. This had been surgically removed, and J. had had a course of radiotherapy followed by chemotherapy. At this point she had had all the therapy which it was possible to give. She was suffering from spread of the cancer cells into the peritoneal cavity and into the pleural cavity, and there were massive effusions of fluid at both sites. She had an abdomen the size of a football and was attending hospital at three weekly intervals for the fluid to be drained off. Her expectation of life would have been about three to four months.

She first came to me in July, along with her husband. We talked together about the nature of cancer — how cancer cells appeared in all of us and how the body tried to control them, and how, in some people, this control process could be interfered with through emotional stress and faulty life styles. We spoke about her own life from her earliest days. J. had been a school teacher, and had recently reached the age of retirement. She felt lost without her daily commitment to her pupils, and her life was now centred around her daughter. Here lay the source of her trouble. Her daughter was an epileptic, and like many epileptics she was unstable and unpredictable in her behaviour. She lived with her parents and was unable to hold down a job. J. felt extremely guilty over this, and blamed herself for her daughter's condition. She was also deeply anxious over what the future might hold for the daughter when she was no longer there to look after her and care for her. Guilt and fear predominated in her emotional state.

At her first visit we talked about the damaging effect of these emotions, and how they stimulated an over production of steroid hormones in the body which upset the working of her immune system. We also spoke of how the relaxation response could lessen these effects, and thus help to get her immune systems working again. She learned a simple system of meditation and visual imaging, and was instructed in nutrition and vitamin and mineral therapy. On her subsequent visits we went further into the problems of guilt and apprehension for the future. She came gradually to see that whatever might be the situation today, it could not be helped by dwelling on the past. The past was past and could not be changed, however much she might wish to do so. In any case epilepsy was not brought about by anything that she might have done — or omitted to do, but that epileptics are acutely sensitive to the thoughts and feelings of those around them, and her own very natural anxieties only served to worsen the position. This was something that she had to learn to accept. We spoke, too, of the importance of her own attitudes and beliefs in determining her own future. If she expected that she would progress rapidly downhill towards inevitable death, then her body would programme itself towards this end. We discussed, also, the meaning of death, not as sheer extinction, but as a transition from one environment to another, and how life had to be seen as a series of opportunities for learning and for making personal growth. All these hazards and traumas of life were no more than exercises in the text book of life, and renewed opportunities for growth. We spoke about loving, and how it was necessary to learn to love oneself, since without loving oneself, and respecting one's own true worth, it was impossible to love others. We spoke of God's individual love and care for all his creatures, and how all things, in the end, worked together for good, even though we could not recognise it at the time. We spoke of the necessity for forgiveness, and how it was necessary to extend that forgiveness to ourselves as well as to others.

I also introduced J. to our own cancer support group at this time, and she and her husband used to travel every other week all the way from London to attend. Here she was in contact with others with similar problems, and here she could share her experience with them and learn from the way in which they handled their problems. She found the conducted group meditations to be a tremendous help, and she experienced for the very first time the peace that such meditations can bring, and the power of prayerful healing through the laying on of hands. Little by little J. started to improve. The amounts of fluid drawn off at the hospital became steadily less and less, and the intervals between became longer and longer. Eventually there came a 'dry tap' when nothing came at all, and she heard her surgeon whisper to the nursing sister, "I don't know what is going on in there, but I am sure it is nothing but good!" Christmas came and went — a Christmas that she had never been expected to see. The atmosphere within the family improved and the daughter's behaviour became better as the weeks went by.

By February J. had improved so much and was making such progress with her meditation that I suggested to her that she might like to come to a week-long conference on meditation which was to be held during May on the island of Iona off the west coast of Scotland. Now Iona is a very special island. It was at one time a centre for Druid worship, and later, following the arrival of the Irish monk, Columba, in the sixth century, became a Christian centre, from which the monks travelled out to preach the gospel of Christ throughout the whole of Scotland and England and into darkest Europe. (The canton of St. Gall, in Switzerland, is actually named after one of Columba's monks, who travelled there to Christianise the local tribesmen.) Myths and legends abound about Iona, and the island was, and remains a centre of spiritual power, and one of the supremely holy places of the western world. J. was fascinated by the idea and readily agreed to attend the conference.

Like many such centres of spiritual power, access to Iona is difficult, and the journey there long and arduous. It entails 600 miles by road, some of it across wild and difficult terrain. There then follows a 45 minute journey by boat, a further hour by bus across the island of Mull, and, finally, a further journey in a tiny open boat across the mile wide Sound of Iona. It is, in every sense of the word, a pilgrimage. Samuel Johnson, the great lexicographer of the eighteenth century, is reported by his biographer, Boswell, as having fallen on his knees and kissed the soil on landing, as he uttered his famous words: "That man is little to be envied whose patriotism would not grow stronger upon the fields of Marathon, or whose piety would not grow warmer amongst the ruins of Iona."

J. made the journey along with her husband. She was still not walking very well, and so they took with them a folding wheel chair in which she was pushed about the island in the intervals during the conference. (The whole island is not more than three miles long, and there are no cars and virtually no roads.) She attended all the talks and meditations, together with the services at the restored but ancient abbey, which are a feature of all Iona conferences. When the end of the conference came and it was time to go home, J. didn't want to go. What she wanted above all else was to visit the legendary Fingal's cave, which is reported to have inspired the composer Mendelssohn to compose his Hebridean Journey. Now Fingal's Cave is on the island of Staffa, an outcrop of black basaltic rock, sticking out of the sea. It lies six rather stormy miles distant from Iona, and the only means of access is in a small open boat. There is no proper landing stage, just some rough rocks, to which the boat ties up, and often it is not possible even to land. J. was lucky, however, since the sea was relatively calm, and she was able to land. She made her way along the narrow cliff path, often no more than half a metre wide, with the sea washing close beneath it, and into the depth of the cave, to hear the echo and to view the stupendous sight of the light coming through the jagged outline of its entrance. She then made her way back to the boat, but, having got there, nothing would content her but that she should climb the hundred and fifty feet to the top of the island to look at the nesting seabirds. (It must be remembered that she had been going around in a wheel chair during the preceding week!) At length honour was satisfied and she returned to the boat, and, the next day, by easy stages, to her home outside London.

It was, by this time, the end of May, eleven months after she had first come to see me, and J. was better than she had been throughout the past two years. She continued to visit me in Norfolk and to make progress, until, sadly, six weeks later, the oil crisis erupted, and the price of petrol escalated so much that they were unable to afford to travel the 200 miles necessary to attend the Norfolk group. She continued with her diet and her meditation, but, lacking the regular healing, from this moment she started to go downhill. In October her condition had deteriorated to such a degree that her husband was no longer able to look after her properly, and she was admitted to the palliative care ward of the hospital she had been attending. She knew that she was dying, but she remained radiant and undaunted at the imminence of death. Shortly before Christmas she took part in a television programme along with another patient, two young doctors and two of the nurses, in which she spoke of the approach of death, and of her firm belief that consciousness went on beyond the death of the body. To her death was a door which opened to another dimension of continued being without the inconvenience of bodily impairment. She had no fear; only a serene and radiant tranquillity. This intensely moving programme materially altered the lives of many who saw it and brought a new understanding of the meaning of death.

By all the normal criteria of medical assessment the case of J. would be considered a failure, and an emphatic proof that the holistic approach does not work. In my view this is wrong, and is based upon an incomplete understanding of the true nature of man and of the place occupied by the physical body. To me, the story of J. is a beautiful and outstanding example of what true healing really is. Even by the most superficial standards of assessment J.'s life had been extended for a year beyond its normal expectation, having regard to her condition when she first visited me. That year had been one of almost unalloyed joy and happiness, in which she had achieved a quality of living which had previously been beyond her. She had come to terms with her problems and accepted them. She died with dignity, an example to all.

S. is another of my patients. She came to me about four years ago with a lump in the breast, in the hopes that surgery might be avoided. The lump was plainly malignant, but there was no sign of any spread to glandular involvement. I told her that in my opinion surgery was necessary, but that provided she was willing to follow the holistic path, it should not be necessary to do more than remove the cancerous lump. She should, therefore, read through the small print of the operation consent form and scratch out anything which allowed the surgeon discretion to do more than remove the lump. She would probably have a battle about this, but after all it was her body, and she had a right to say what was to be done to it. S. was admitted and had her lump removed. Her breast was spared, and her husband, to whom the cosmetic part of mastectomy was all important, was delighted. Unfortunately (with hindsight) S. was given a post-operative course of radiotherapy to the breast tissue, as a sort of precaution against recurrence, and this was later to prove a minor disaster. (Radiotherapy to the chest area can damage the all important thymus gland, through which the T-lymphocytes must pass, and thus result in a lowering of immune efficiency.)

The background to S.'s cancer was a familiar one. Coming from an emotionally starved family background, she had met and married her young husband while in her early twenties. Physically she was slim and boyish and relatively undeveloped from the feminine aspect. She had no maternal interests and neither she nor her husband had any desire for children. She shared his life and interests and was completely subservient to him, with no friends or interests of her own. She worked as a secretary in a firm of estate agents, where she was the central figure in the running of the office. She had an excellent relationship with her boss, and was regarded with affection and friendship. She was equally attached to her work and to him and found fulfilment in her competent efficiency and the reliance which was placed upon her. Trouble began when this relationship began to deteriorate. Though she did not recognise it at the time, her boss was an immature and somewhat inadequate personality, and with arrival of another girl in the office, S.'s key position began to be undermined. She was losing her all important role in life, and once this was gone, would have had no individual life of her own, and been left in subservience to her husband. Although she did not recognise this at the time, it was clearly the trigger point for the cancer. Part of her wanted "out" from this unacceptable life situation. There had to be change. Cancer, leading to death, was one way of achieving this, though a rather drastic way!

In the course of the counselling sessions, we explored this together, and S. came to see that the office role was, at the moment, of supreme importance to her as a means of expressing her own individuality and worth. She must therefore, instead of feeling resentful, at the behaviour of her employer, view this with compassionate indulgence, and seek to rebuild the former relationship of confident trust and reliance which had meant so much to her. Alongside this, however, she must seek to develop a life and interests of her own, and be less subservient to her husband. She did exactly this, and for over two years things went well and there was no further trouble. Some time later, however, history repeated itself, and there was further trouble in the office, and S. was threatened with the loss of her job. This fuelled another breakdown in her immune system and she developed another lump in the self-same breast. This time she was not lucky (or was it the immuno-destructive effect of the radiotherapy which she had undergone?), for by the time she saw me, there was involvement of a lymph gland, and I had reluctantly to tell her that this time I felt that mastectomy was necessary if she was to avoid the risk of future recurrence.

Bravely S. went ahead with this. She is not a very feminine person, and the contours of her breast had never meant a great deal to her. Her husband, however, is devastated, and will, as she puts it, "have nothing to do with her above the waist!" All the loving tenderness of intimacy has been completely destroyed, (if, indeed, it was ever there, which I am beginning to doubt), and he is unable even to look at what he regards as a mutilated body. S., in the meantime, has regarded this as a challenge to be overcome. She has rebuilt the situation in the office with regard to her boss, and is now content and happy in her work. She has started to take an intense interest in healing and the holistic approach. This has brought her out from the closed environment of her home into contact with others of similar interests. She has started to attend seminars and groups, and in so doing has made friends of her own. She has discovered an interest in music, both in listening and making music. She has brought a musical instrument and taking lessons, she has just passed the first of her grade examinations in her instrument. She has also started taking lessons in the theory of music, and intends later to take a more advanced instrument and try to join an orchestra. In the course of all this she has found an understanding of life, and a wide compassion which is able to embrace the inadequacies of her husband. The whole of life has taken on a new meaning for her, and she is truly one who says, "Thank God for my cancer! It is the best thing that could have happened to me. I have learned so much from it and have met so many people that I would never have had a chance to meet and to learn from, had I not developed cancer." S. continues to be well. She follows her meditation and her diet, and attends regularly at a support group for cancer sufferers, where her example is an inspiration to others just starting on the path. So long as she continues in her present state of calm and serenity, and to express her own essential self in her life, she will, I am sure, continue to be well. But the fact that she had a relapse tells us that she is at risk, and will have to continue on guard for a very long time.

P. is another patient of mine. I first met her when she brought her husband, who was then in the terminal stages of leukaemia, to see me. At this point he was so weak and ill that he could hardly walk, and had to hold on to the furniture to get about the house. He had had innumerable courses of chemotherapy, and no more therapy was possible. In desperation P. made contact on the telephone with a spiritual healer, whose name she obtained from, of all places!, the

Citizens' Advice Bureau. He told her that he would send absent healing through prayer and concentration to her husband at a particular time that evening. She said nothing to him about this, feeling, instinctively, that he would not wish to have anything to do with what he would probably regard as the occult. Shortly before the appointed time, P. and her three adolescent children were sitting together when her husband dragged himself into the room, saying that he was just going to try and get a breath of fresh air in the garden. He was walking with extreme difficulty and weakness. Ten minutes later the family were shattered to see him return, brisk and upright, walking at his old pace, as if he had never been ill in his life. His face wore a somewhat puzzled expression. "It's an extraordinary thing," he said, "but something happened when I was out there in the garden. Quite suddenly I felt well again, like I used to do, before all this began. I just can't understand it." At this point P. told him what she had done. "Well, he said, "if spiritual healing can do that, there can't be much wrong with it. Let's have some more!"

So P. rang up the healer to tell him the result and ask him where to go from there. Now, as it happened, he was a friend of mine, and we had just recently returned together from one of the conferences held on Iona — on healing. So P. and her husband came to me. This was early on in my work, and I had not then developed the counselling and psychotherapy patterns which I now use in cancer, so the husband was instructed just in meditation and visualisation, and in diet. He also attended regularly at our own cancer healing and meditation group. Although he was plainly far past the "point of no return" things started to happen. He accepted the fact that he was ill and unable to continue his work. (Basically he was a "workaholic", who had brought his work into the hospital and turned his bedside into an extension of his office bringing his secretary and a telephone to help him! He had no life outside his work, and this was probably the background to his illness.) Instead he took over the running of the house and the preparation of the meals. Every day he would cycle down to the city to buy the fruit and vegetables needed, and prepare luscious and appetising vegetarian meals for himself and all the family, while his wife continued at her job. He was completely happy and fulfilled in this. The pair of them were even able to resume a sexual relationship, which had not been possible for a couple of years. The end came with dramatic suddenness. He caught a summer cold. There was no resistance to this, owing to the many courses of chemotherapy he had undergone, and within two days this had turned to bronchopneumonia. Despite being admitted to hospital and being pumped full of antibiotics, there was no capacity for resistance left. The immune system had been completely destroyed, and he died, fully conscious to the last, in thirty-six hours.

P. was deeply affected at his death. However, she found strength and support through continuing to attend the support group and receiving healing there. She went on with her job and gradually started to resume her old interests of amateur theatricals and operatics. In due course she met another man, to whom she became deeply attached. (Her husband had always said that if she wished to, she should marry again.) He, however, was married, and there seemed no prospect of a divorce. After some years of being together, he told her just before Christmas, that as there seemed to be no prospect of marriage, they could no longer continue the relationship. P. was devastated. "I felt," she said, "that it was not worth going on with life. I just wanted to die!" This state of mind continued for several weeks, and shortly after, P. discovered a lump in her breast. She at once called to see me. I told her that she must see a surgeon, and that, if the lump was considered to be cancerous, and having regard both to the nature of the lump and the story that she had told me, I thought that it very probably was, the lump should be surgically removed, but that on no account were they to be allowed to remove her breast. P.'s account of her meeting with her surgeon is hilarious. He was furious. "In six months' time," he told her, "you will come screaming to me to take your breast off, and it will be too late. Damn it all, woman," he went on, "if your car has a faulty carburettor, you don't tell the mechanic what to do. You tell him to fix it!" "Yes, Doctor," she replied, "but there is a difference between my body and my car! After all, my car can't tell me what is wrong with it. Nor can it heal the scratches in its paint work! My body can do both of these. It's really not the same thing at all.''

Greatly to his displeasure she stuck to her guns. Only the lump was to be removed, and there was to be no follow-up of radiotherapy. She would do the follow-up herself through diet, relaxation, meditation and healing. Unfortunately, in the period prior to operation her family doctor had taken a "needle biopsy" of the lump. (Needle biopsy consists in sticking a needle attached to a syringe into the tumour and withdrawing a few cells for microscopic analysis. It is a highly dangerous procedure, which by penetrating the surrounding wall of fibrous tissue by which the body attempts to isolate and contain the tumour, often permits the escape of stray cells along the track of the needle.) It was so in P.'s case. A few weeks' later a small gland, the first in the lymphatic drainage chain became enlarged. Nothing daunted, P. set to work to deal with this through her meditation and her visualisation. To her delight, she found that she was able to do this, and the gland so shrank in size as to be hardly palpable. Moreover, she found that she could use this as a sort of barometer. If she allowed herself to feel under pressure, or diverged from her strictly regulated diet it would increase in size. When she corrected the faulty influences, it receded again. On the occasion of a holiday in the Greek Islands this year, when she says she allowed herself to deviate from her vegetarian diet, she found that the peace and tranquillity of the environment more than compensated for any dietary deviations, and by the time she returned home she was unable to feel it. Obviously P. will have to remain on guard for a considerable time. Her experience, however, demonstrates very clearly the working of the holistic method.

K. is another who has found healing of her cancer through her own determination and refusal to lie down and die. K.'s husband was dying of cancer of the oesophagus, a peculiarly unpleasant and distressing form of cancer. While she was nursing him she discovered a lump in her breast — not altogether surprising in view of what we have discovered about the impact of personal loss upon the working of the immune system. By the time that she felt free to go for medical advice this had grown to such a degree that it had ulcerated through the skin. Her surgeon told her that she would have to have a mastectomy, followed by intensive radiation and chemotherapy. Even then the prognosis was poor. Instinctively K. felt that this was not the road for her and she started to look for other ways of dealing with her problems. She went to America. Here she saw another surgeon. His treatment of her was insensitive and even cruel. He told her in great detail what he considered was likely to happen to her if she did not agree to undergo surgery. Not only would the cancer become progressively larger and more destructive until most of her breast would be eaten away and replaced by a foul, fungating mass, but she would develop secondary deposits in the spine, the pelvis and the ribs which would result in increasing pain and disability, until eventually she would die in misery. Again K. refused to accept this prognosis. She went to see the Simontons, and, after return home to the Bristol Cancer Help Centre. She determined that she was going to heal herself, no matter what it cost her. She started out by taking the grape cure, which involves living for six weeks upon nothing but grapes. (This method is by no means suitable for everyone, and is to be approached with caution. It also depends upon a regular supply of large quantities of fresh, sun-ripened grapes, which is by no means easy to ensure, especially as the grapes must be free from any form of chemical contamination,) She followed this up by a six weeks' fast upon the Breuss fruit and vegetable juices. She also practised deep relaxation, meditation and visual imaging. To her delight the cancer began to shrink and the skin to heal. She finally went on to a completely vegetarian diet, with complete abstinence from refined carbohydrates, eggs and dairy produce. Her cancer is now completely healed and she has remained free from any complications for the past four years. She has started a small group for helping cancer patients and is a regular speaker upon "The Gentle Way with Cancer" at workshops and seminars.

A word of caution is necessary at this point. Very few persons have the dedication and determination to follow the path which K. followed. The healing of her cancer is due at least as much to her personal qualities as to the methods which she used to heal herself. But it shows what can happen when the immune system is intact and undisturbed by emotional and psychological factors. Moreover breast cancers vary considerably in their level of activity and capacity for metastasis. I personally would hesitate very much before advising any patient of mine to follow such a course.

B. is not a patient of mine, and consequently I am not familiar with the preceding patterns in her life. None the less the story of her cancer and its healing is of profound importance to all cancer sufferers. The following account is abridged from her article in "Harmony", the official journal of the Association for New Approaches to Cancer.

"In 1977 at the age of 51 I was admitted to hospital for investigations. It was thought that I had a small clot in my brain, which would be simple to deal with. I casually mentioned that I had a lump in my breast which my doctor thought was a cyst. The hospital doctor said that they should do a biopsy on the breast lump. The result of the biopsy proved that the lump in my breast was cancerous. My whole body was then scanned. Secondary growths were found in my ribs and spine and further brain tests showed that what I had was a malignant brain tumour. I was told that the disease had gone too far to be cured. Surgery would not help, and the new drugs would only cause severe side effects and would not help. I asked how long I had to live. "You should be all right for two to three years before anything drastic happens" came the reply. "Then what?" said I. "We will not let you suffer", was the answer. I thought to myself, "Two years — we'll make it three. Good, I have that much time to work on getting well."

"While in hospital", B. goes on, "I had two spiritual experiences which left a deep impression. In what is known as an out-of-the-body experience my consciousness slipped out of my body and, in fact, I was looking down at it as it lay in bed. I thought I looked pretty scruffy, with my hair uncombed, but then I realized that it was not important. Then I thought that I was dead and had not made a will. Again the realization came, "It is not important." Immediately after this

I heard a voice which said, "No, you are not dead, you are being tried. There is more come and you must smile for the sake of others as they do not understand."

"I woke mext morning full of love for everyone and everything. My friends, the Atlanteans, a healing group, came to see me and promised to give me distant healing every day. I thought I would tune in to this healing. During the night I woke with the feeling that I might hear the voice that had spoken to me after my out-of-the-body experience. To my disappointment I didn't, so I just waited. Suddenly I felt an electric shock that practically lifted me off the bed, and I realized that I had been healed and was not going to die, but also that I still had to help myself." . . .

B. went home after treatment, having been warned that she would lose her hair as the result of the radiation. She also became very weak, but as the result of the steroid she was taking her weight increased until she was seven kilos above her normal weight. One night she had a dream in which she was told that she must either go to see a well-known nature cure, doctor, whom she had consulted in the past, or else visit a particular naturopath. She decided to visit the naturopath. At this time she was so weak that she had to be carried into the clinic, and the naturopath, whom I know personally, told me that he was very worried that she might even die before he could get her out of the clinic! Despite this, he agreed to give treatment for a three weeks' trial period. At the end of this period, finding that B. had a strongly positive attitude, he agreed to continue with treatment.

"For the first two weeks of his "treatment," B. goes on, "I lived on juices only, in order to get my body detoxified. Then I was put on a modified Gerson Diet, which consists of fruit and vegetables only, with no meat, eggs, dairy products, salt, tea, coffee, alcohol or processed foods. I knew that I had to follow Mr. E.'s advice and treatment as closely as possible, although this was very difficult indeed. As I was very weak, my friends, the Atlanteans, took turns to take me to the clinic to see Mr. E. every week, for six months. Without telling the Cobalt Clinic I gradually reduced the high doses of steroids until I came off them completely.

"Mr. E.'s treatment also included mega-vitamins, minerals and enzymes, plus the use of a special dia-pulse machine which speeds up healing. I meditated every day, visualizing the cancer shrinking and my body defences getting stronger."

(The Gerson diet in its strict form insists upon organically grown fruit and vegetables. It is also not thought to be suitable for patients who have had conventional treatment with radiation therapy or drugs, and strictly trained Gerson practitioners will not accept such patients. Mr. E., however, does not insist upon these conditions and accepts cancer patients who have had orthodox treatments.)

"My fight to survive was hard going. I spent most of the time moving from bathroom to kitchen to settee and back again. Every hour, on the hour, I had to prepare and drink fresh fruit and vegetable juices; every hour on the half hour I had to have a coffee enema to stimulate the production of bile which in turn helps to remove toxins rapidly. (N.B. Coffee enemas can now be replaced by taking an infusion of herbs, which has the same effect in stimulating the liver.) Fresh salads and a special soup had to be prepared, too. Over a period of six weeks I was too weak to have a bath or to change and make my bed. Sometimes I felt the walls were closing in on me, or that something was crawling right inside my head, although I knew, of course, that this wasn't so. There were times when I was temporarily paralysed. The healing process produced some tiresome side effects, such as skin rashes, small septic spots, intense itching and cramp. Although these symptoms were highly unpleasant, I welcomed them because they meant that the toxins were rapidly coming out of my body.

"During my weak spell I picked up a virus in my eye which resulted in an ulcerated cornea. Mr. E.'s dia-pulse machine worked wonders in clearing up the trouble. The final side effect was a deep abscess over my right kidney, for which I had to have an operation under general anaesthetic.

"I stayed on the Gerson diet and Mr. E.'s treatment for eighteen months. Since that time I have had several scans and I have been pronounced clear of cancer. I feel better than I had felt before falling ill. My feeling of love for everyone remains. There is no bitterness, depression or fear in me. I stick to my wholesome vegetarian diet, except for occasionally eating a small portion of chicken or white fish. All in all I could not be happier, and I thank everyone who had been concerned with my survival and recovery. I do hope my story will encourage others.''

Three years ago I shared a platform with B. and can testify to her energy and present glowing health, which she uses in trying to help other cancer sufferers around where she lives. Her healing was undoubtedly the result of her own courage and tenacity in the face of quite incredible difficulties. At this time far less was known and understood about the psycho-somatic factors in cancer, and, apart from the skill and expertise of Mr. E., the naturopath, B. had to go it alone and find her own way through. I am also firmly convinced that her difficulties were made immensely greater by the concen-trated course of radiation which she had undergone. Radia-tion, like chemotherapy, is of value in emergency. It helps to buy time. But there is a price to be paid. It damages white cell production in the body, and further depresses the immune/ rejection system, and it is always a matter calling for very nice judgement to determine exactly where the balance of benefit lies. Sadly this judgement is not always exercised.

Another very interesting aspect of B.'s story is her experience of healing and of her out-of-the-body experience. O.B.E.s, as they are known, are well documented in the literature of the paranormal, though they are less well known amongst doctors. They offer suggestive and powerful evidence for the view that mind and body, while closely interlinked during life, are intrinsically different, and that consciousness is not dependent upon brain cell activity, but merely makes use of the brain as a transducer of energy to become expressed in the material dimension. Moreover healing, whether through direct contact, or as in the case of B., at a distance, is a more common phenomenon than is currently recognised, and, in the opinion of the writer, forms an important part of the holistic package. Its effect, as in the case of B., who awoke next morning convinced that she had been healed and was not going to die, takes place, in most instances, initially at the mental or even the spiritual level, becoming apparent later at the physical level provided that the self-healing power in the body has not been irretrievably damaged. It probably works through an amplification of this power of self-healing. (C.f. Alexis Carrel's account in "Man the Unknown".) Both of these phenomena, and their relationship to the medical and spiritual fields are discussed in full in the author's book "The Gate of Healing".

Working with the Holistic Approach is never easy. It calls for very special qualities in the therapist, and a sense of commitment and dedication on the part of the patient, which not every patient possesses. It takes great courage and motivation to accept that your illness is something that you are doing to yourself, and that the first thing required, if you want to be well, is to stop doing it! Moreover, many people, though paying lip-service to this, do not really want to be healed. For them illness, especially cancer, may be a way of getting what they really want from life; a face saving excuse for failure; a way of constraining others to what we want; a way out from a situation which can no longer be tolerated; or even a way of expiating our own feelings of guilt and self blame. The following example is an illustration of the latter situation.

H. was a young and lovely woman in her early thirties. She came with her husband following having had a mastectomy for a breast cancer, which had been followed by radiation and chemotherapy. The cancer however was still active and she wanted to try to help herself. The young couple were obviously extremely happy and deeply attached to each other. H. had come from a fairly typical background, with emotional deprivation in childhood, a strongly self-critical attitude, and great reticence over her emotional side. She was very ready to embrace the diet, to try to meditate and to visualise, and to take part in the healing group and receive healing. She was a lot less ready to share her thoughts and emotions during the counselling periods, and I felt from the start that there was something very important that she was keeping back. She made very little improvement, and was soon undergoing yet a further course of chemotherapy, to which there was no response. After a very few months she had to be admitted to hospital for terminal care. While in hospital she was visited regularly by another member of the group, the wife of a healed lung cancer patient. "God is punishing me for what I have done, isn't he?" she said. And then the whole pitiful story, the story which she had been so ashamed to share, came out. She was the second wife of her husband. She had met him and fallen deeply in love with him while he was still married to his first wife, and she had set out to marry him. She had been the occasion of the break-up of his first marriage, and much as in the story of David and Bathsheba, she had then married him after the divorce. It wasn't God who was punishing her. It was her own guilty conscience. It was her feelings of guilt and self-blame, which she was totally unable to handle. Had she been able to speak of this when she first came, it might have been possible to teach her how to forgive herself; to explain that marriages just do not break up unless there is a crack in their structure. Had there been complete harmony and unity in the husband's first marriage, she might have thrown out all the lures she could think of, and he would never even have noticed them. The marriage must have been unstable in the first place for the divorce ever to have happened, and, in all probability, the first wife was at least as much to blame, and probably far more so. Armed with this knowledge she might have learned how to forgive herself. Sadly her disease proceeded apace to its inevitable conclusion. I hope that she is at peace.

This sad little story underlines some of the difficulties in working with the holistic approach. Counsellors and phychotherapists have to be persons of quite exceptional maturity and deeply spiritual understanding. They have to have the intuitive ability to sense when their patients are holding back, and to be able to inspire and motivate the patient towards recovery. They also need to be able to sense when the patient does not want to be healed. Many patients come to me because their relatives want them to do so. Their loved ones attempt to impose upon them the duty of being healed. Sometimes this is the last thing that they really want. It is necessary always for the therapist to realise that the choice of life or death belongs to the patient, and only to the patient. It is his/her right to make that choice, and we have to be able to sense what that choice really is. It is also the duty of the therapist to ensure that the choice is made from a standpoint of knowledge and understanding on the part of the patient, and his task to help impart that knowledge and understanding. Thus the therapist must be one who has faced and come to terms with the fact of death, the one sure thing in the life of every single person. For at that point, when the patient has decided that the struggle is no longer worth the effort; when the cry goes up, "Stop the world. I want to get off!"; when the delights of the Elysian Fields outweigh the traumas and ephemeral pleasures of the world, the therapist must be able to go to where the patient is, and to hold his/her hand and lead him on the way. At that point we cease to make hard demands upon our patients. We stop insisting on changes in diet and life styles and pose instead the question: "What must you do to bless the world before you go? Is there anyone whom you still need to forgive? Have you anything for which you have to forgive yourself?"

To do this successfully we need to have worked upon ourselves. We must have faced the deep questions of our own mortality, and the meaning of life and death. We must have found our answer. The next chapter tells of how one cancer sufferer did just this, and finding them has been enabled to help her fellows.

CHAPTER 4

Cancer as a Transformational Experience

There are now many people who have experienced cancer, and who have fought and won their battle against it. When one talks to these people, one thing is immediately apparent. They are no longer quite the same people as they were when they developed the cancer. For them, cancer has been a process of personal transformation. They no longer have the same attitudes to life, nor the same sense of values. Life has attained a new dimension and a new direction. Many of them say quite openly, "My cancer has been the best thing that has ever happened to me, and I would not trade this experience for anything that you could offer me." A young patient of mine once said in a radio interview, when asked how she viewed the experience of cancer through which she had passed: "Well, at the time it was absolutely terrifying. But when I look back on it today, I can see that it was enormously enriching."

It has been said by one famous cancer specialist that cancer is an invitation to change your whole approach to living. It starts with the fact that we can choose whether we want to live or to die. Most people will reply at once: "Of course I do not want to die. I have far too much living to do." We may know that life seems awfully tough, and may even wonder whether it is worth the struggle to go on, but it is very rarely that we shall say, "I would rather be dead than go on like this." It is far more likely that we shall be saying, "Why should this have to happen to me? What have I done to deserve this terrible disease?" But at this point it is important to ask ourselves the question: "It is just possible that there is some little part of me that wants to escape from life as it is or as it has been? Even though I have a great many reasons to go on living, can it be that there is a part of me that wants out of life? A part of me that has 'had it'?" Very often the answer to this will be "Yes", but we shall have hidden this unpalatable fact away beneath the carpet of our subconscious.

As we have seen, there are a number of causative factors, which operate all the time in our bodies to produce cancer. But, on the whole, our bodies manage to deal extremely efficiently with all sorts of abnormal substances, even cancer cells, all through our lives. It is only when something happens to interfere with this marvellous mechanism for self-repair that cancer develops. Very often this 'something' is a weakening of the will-to-live, and this seems to be the last straw which has broken the back of the camel. So at this point when a person develops cancer, it is necessary to stop and ask the question, "Why did I develop cancer at this particular moment? What might be its personal meaning for me? Is it telling me that I need to make a change in my life?"

If it is, then one way of making such a change from an unfulfilling pattern of life would be to allow the condition to proceed to death. This is certainly a change — but rather a drastic one! It may be that beneath the conscious awareness that seems to want to go on living, (perhaps because it is afraid of dying), there is a deep understanding that the present pattern of life is unfulfilling and frustrating, and is in need of radical revision. Many of us deeply believe that consciousness is deathless, and continues beyond physical death. In that case, death is a perfectly acceptable answer to the wish for change, and the unfulfilling path that we are on may be leading us towards death as a means of effecting the desired change.

But there is another choice. If, deep down within ourselves, we realise that we have been tied to old patterns of acting and reacting; if we understand that the motions of life we have been going through no longer have any meaning for us; that there are important parts of ourselves that are no longer finding expression in freedom and joyfulness; that old patterns and values are holding us down and preventing us from finding a wider view of true reality; if the pain of the loss of a dear and valued relationship has left us helpless and hopeless; if these, or anything else, obstruct the expression of our lives, then we can choose whether to change the pattern of life, or to continue within it.

The right to make this choice is ours, and ours alone. No one can impose that choice upon us. If our choice is to continue on the old pathway, then that is quite all right. The choice, and the right to make it, is ours even if the consequence of the choice is physical death. We shall continue our spiritual journey, and the learning will go on.

But we can make another choice, if we want to do so. If we **really** want to, we can choose to make a deep, fulfilling, expanding change in the pattern of our life while we are still alive in our physical bodies. Whichever choice we make there is a real transformation. But the choice lies between physical and spiritual death. The 'spiritual death' is the change which we make in the pattern of our lives. (It is interesting here to reflect that St Paul, who was very aware of all this, actually spoke of 'dying to sin' and being 'born again into eternal life'. By sin, of course, he meant the old, unfulfilling patterns of life, unrelating to ourselves, our fellow men and the universe.) If we can make this choice, and let go of the old patterns, then new life is born within us. We no longer need cancer, or death, to bring about this change. We have found another way to bring about the transformation.

If you are faced with the need to make this change, here is an exercise which you can do. Just supposing that your fairy godmother were to appear and make you a once-in-a-lifetime offer: that in six months time your life can be anything that you want. What would you tell her? What would your reply be? Do you even know? If you do know, what are you doing to bring this about? If you do not know, do you think that it is important? If you do know, what it is in you that is blocking your movement towards the sort of life that you really want? These are important questions, which you must try to answer. You have to find your own special music, and sing your own special song, if you would be truly well. There are three objections which are commonly advanced to singing one's own song. One is that it will be so bad, that it will be unacceptable to oneself. Another is that it will be unacceptable to others. A third is that it will be so full of contradictions that it could not possibly exist. Which of these is yours? What is it that is blocking your way forward?

To heal yourself, you have to mobilise your resources of healing. That is what the book is all about. There are three reasons why people want to be healed of cancer. One is: "I am against it. I am afraid of dying and of illness. In any case, there are far too many things that I want to do. I have too much unfinished business in my life." The second is: "I want things to be like they were before I became ill." The third is: "I want to sing my own unique and special song. I want to make my life what it truly ought to be." The body will not mobilise its resources of healing for the first two reasons. At times it will fight for its life for the sake of someone else, but when that need is past, it will give up the struggle. At that point the condition will flare up, and run away out of control. Thus change of attitude is vital, if healing is to ensue. This means very often that we have to adjust ourselves to life, and stop trying to adjust life to ourselves. We have to learn to behave in a way that is so right for ourselves that we have no time to be angry or resentful any more. We have to recognise that we have needs both for privacy and solitude in our relationships with other persons. But the balance between privacy and relationships will vary with each person, and we have to find exactly the right balance for ourselves. It means, also having as fierce and tender a concern for ourselves as we have for those whom we love. In the healing of cancer this is vital.

We have to learn to forgive ourselves as well as others. So here is another exercise for each one of us. What do we have to do, or obtain, in order fully to forgive ourselves? Secondly, what are we forgiving ourselves for? We must each think long and carefully over this, for it will help us to pass through this process of transformation. Again, just supposing that what is said by some people is actually true, that reincarnation is a fact, and that life is a spiritual school, what lessons do we think we have come here to learn in this life? If we can answer these questions we will know far more about ourselves, and be on the way to transforming our own lives, and finding our own particular music to sing.

Here is an example of a life pattern of a patient who has had cancer, and which might be described in the following way. (I am indebted to my friend, Francis Horn, Ph.D. for this extract.)

> "The pattern is looking to other people to supply validation for my own life. The pattern is expecting other people to meet my standards, and giving them trouble when they do not. The pattern is expecting other people to meet my expectations, and **feeling** very strongly when they do not — feeling such as anger, frustration, no love, deep depression, despair. The pattern is projecting my expectations into the outside world, and demanding that it meet them for me, as the only real means to validate myself. This means that when I allow this pattern to take over, I let other people, circumstances, events determine my whole state of being, including my health and my happiness.
>
> "I can continue to do this if I choose. I can look at where it gets me, and I can decide whether I wish to go on with it or not. But I now see that I have another option. If I wish, I can stop looking outside myself, and I can look directly into myself, my central core, my heart, and let everything radiate out from that. I can trust my intuitive knowing, this deep intuition, as the 'guiding component of my beingness', which places me on a fulfilling path. As I do this, I find that I am being myself; I can let other people be who and what they really are. I see that the way to change, to transform, to move into a much more fulfilling and harmonious state of well-being, energy, joy, lies within my own consciousness. Inwardly I choose to attune to something greater than I am; I flow in the most creative, life-giving direction I can see, moment by moment, and this makes me feel part of the whole, which is sustaining me and all that is."

That is the experience of one person confronted with cancer. When she searched out the hitherto unfaced will to die in a part of herself, and focussed on life-long patterns of life, which had seemed to serve her well, she discovered that these, when seen in the light of life-or-death situation, needed deep, radical change. When she made this change, letting go of all previously held patterns in order to follow a free flow through her spirit, her mind and her body, of the Divine energy, out of which all things are formed, she found the healing of her cancer. She said afterwards that this experience of cancer was the most valuable thing that had ever happened in her life, and that it was something that she would not exchange for all the riches in the world. It has brought her a new understanding and had changed her life in a way that nothing else could ever have done.

The ability to make this change is open to each one of us, if we will. But the ways in which we will need to change will differ in each person, since every one of us is unique, and has had different experiences in our lives. But the need for change remains. No matter in what way our lives are unfulfilled, we must move out from these old, unfulfilling patterns of life, letting go the past in order to allow a new pattern to emerge. In making this change we find a true healing and wholeness. In its train will come radiant and abundant health, and a sense of well-being beyond our wildest dreams. We shall have been transformed. But this transformation is something that we have to do for ourselves. No one, however wise and gifted, can do it for us. They may point the way, and help to hold up a mirror to ourselves, to see ourselves as we really are, with new eyes. They can help us to recognise our own deep needs, and to find our own unique and special music. But the song is ours alone, and we alone can sing it.

CHAPTER 5

Nutrition and Detoxification

NUTRITION

Natural systems of cancer control depend upon the capacity of the body to search out and destroy the cancer cells. This is the function of the immune system and, in particular, of the T-lymphocytes. The activity of the T-lymphocytes is stimulated by the amount of prostaglandin E1, which the body produces. This in turn, can be enhanced or diminished by a number of dietary substances. Thus correct eating habits are CRUCIAL to cancer control. The principles of the diet can be listed as follows:

1. A vegetarian wholefood diet, based upon "living" foodstuffs such as fruit, vegetables, sprouted seeds, grains and pulses has the greatest ability to restore the body. Food should be as fresh as possible, and, with a few exceptions, should be eaten raw. Most good food of plant origin does not need cooking, only careful preparation.

2. Commercially grown fruit and vegetables are nutritionally deficient, and contaminated with agro-chemicals. Use organic produce, grown on naturally fertilised soil without the use of pesticides and other toxic substances. (In London organic produce can be obtained from The Farm Shop, 1 Neal's Yard, Covent Garden WC1; from Wholefoods, 24 and 31 Paddington Street, W1, and from an increasing number of small wholefood shops. If you live outside London, write to the organic Growers Association, Hon. Sec. Mr. C. Wacher, Aeron Park, Llangeitho, Dyfed, enclosing

SAE for particulars of organic suppliers in your area. Or consult "The Organic Food Guide", by Alan Gear, which covers the U.K., £2.50 from health food shops.)

3. Your food intake should be adequate and nutritionally correct but not rich. Over-eating is dangerous and destructive, and fat consumption decreases prostaglandin production.

4. Salt, salt substitutes and all foodstuffs containing salt MUST be excluded from your diet. You may find this difficult at first, but if you persevere, you will soon begin to enjoy the real flavour of food, which is so often masked by salt. Avoid refined sugar totally, and cut to a minimum your consumption of honey, molasses or any other "natural" sugar. All carbohydrates (i.e. starch- and sugar-containing foods) diminish prostaglandin production and should be drastically cut. Sour and slightly bitter flavours are preferable to sweet. Use good quality cider vinegar lavishly in salad dressings and flavourings; it promotes digestion.

5. What matters in food is NOT its calorie content but its subtle "energy", deriving from a not wholly understood vital force of fresh whole food, of which we are only just becoming aware. This subtle but important quality ebbs away in storage and during the cooking or freezing process. (Some processed foods, such as corn flakes, contain NO vital energy at all.)

6. For that reason ALL PRESERVED AND PROCESSED FOOD IS TOTALLY FORBIDDEN, whether tinned, bottled, smoked, salted, pickled or deep-frozen. (Deep freezing is probably the least damaging form of food preservation, but even here the content of some delicate substances such as pantothenic acid may be reduced by as much as 80% through deep freezing, storing and reconstituting.) Some smoked foods contain in addition certain hydrocarbons, which are cancer-producing. Deep-frozen food is

probably the least unsatisfactory, but even this should only be taken when there is no other alternative. NO artificial flavouring, colouring, preservative or other additive is permitted.

7. Those foods which cannot be eaten raw should be cooked in a way which is least destructive of nutritional values. Do not use pressure cookers, or infra-red ovens, which are highly destructive of important enzymes and vitamins through the increased levels of heat obtainable. Avoid, too, the use of aluminium or lead-containing cooking vessels. Many people have been found to have hidden allergies to aluminium, which is productive of much unrecognised ill health. Stainless steel or enamelled cast iron pots and pans are best. Invest in heavy-bottomed ones with close fitting lids. Vegetables should be cooked slowly and gently in a minimum of water, so as to prevent loss of vital minerals and trace elements. (If the vegetables have been organically grown, the cooking water may be used to enrich soups and stews. Otherwise it should be discarded. Potatoes and root vegetables may be baked in the oven. NO FRIED FOODS ARE PERMITTED. (This is because the intense heat involved in frying produces dangerous hydrocarbons in the fat.)

8. The reason for cutting out animal protein, i.e. meat, poultry, fish and eggs, is that its digestion absorbs the body's production of digestive enzymes which appear to play a vital role in the destruction of cancer deposits. (Egg yolk is also rich in cholesterol, which is an animal fat, and to be avoided.) In addition, commercially produced meat and poultry can contain high levels of toxic chemicals, antibiotics and growth hormones, which must be avoided. Most habitual meat eaters can switch successfully to a well balanced vegetarian diet; this should be done in all cases for the first three months of therapy at least. In the few cases where, after the first three months, meat seems to be essential, it should be eaten in small amounts, not more than twice a week, and only in the form of "white meat", i.e. fish, fresh rabbit, fresh (not deep-frozen)

free-range chicken, and lamb or mutton from organically reared flocks. Beef, pork, bacon, and all forms of cooked meats and sausages should be avoided.

9. Alcohol, tobacco, tea, coffee, cocoa, chocolate, cakes, biscuits, sweets, crisps, peanuts, and soft drinks are totally forbidden.

10. White flour and polished, i.e. white, rice should be avoided. Buy wholemeal flour in small amounts and keep it in the refrigerator to prevent it from becoming rancid. Buy organically grown brown rice and other whole cereals; the commercial varieties often contain concentrations of harmful chemicals in their husks. Porridge, made from organically grown rolled oats, cooked in water without salt and sweetened with a very little honey, makes a fine high-protein breakfast dish. Some cancer patients find rye bread easier to digest than wheat bread.

11. Chemically treated tap water must be avoided. Use pure spring water for drinking and cooking. Invest in a simple water filter for general purposes. In England the Brita Filter, which can be obtained from health food shops, or the Mayrei 2000 filter, which is sold by La Cource de Vie, P.O. box 66, Chichester, West Sussex PO18 9HH are suitable. Spa or Volvic mineral waters are also recommended.

12. Freshly made raw fruit and vegetable juices are a mainstay of most anti-cancer nutritional programmes. You should drink four 250 ml. glasses of fresh carrot juice a day, on its own, or if you prefer it and the flavour is not to your taste, mixed with a small piece of raw beetroot and a fresh raw cooking apple. Bottled, canned or concentrated commercial fruit and vegetable juices cannot be substituted for freshly made ones. The only bottled juice acceptable for cancer patients is Breuss vegetable juice, made by Biotta and sold in health food shops. A book describing the Breuss therapy can be bought from Nuhealth, 9 Magdala Road, Mapperley Park, Nottingham NG3 5DF, price £4.00.

13. Fats of all kinds — butter, margarine, lard, dripping etc, — should be avoided, at least for the first three months of the dietary treatment. Cold-pressed table quality (i.e. made for human consumption) linseed oil can be added to baked potatoes, salads, etc., up to 40 ml. a day. Cold-pressed safflower and olive oil may be used in small amounts. Keep all open bottles of oil in the refrigerator. Even after three months, limit your fat intake to fresh, unsalted butter, in small amounts. This is better than using margarine, which normally contains saturated fatty acids, produced from the polyunsaturates in the manufacturing process.

14. Reduce dairy foods to a minimum, especially during the first three to six months. Milk and cheese contain casein which inhibits prostaglandin production. If you can get it, drink ⅓ litre buttermilk a day. Fresh yoghourt, home made from skimmed milk, can be taken in moderation after the first six months.

15. Eat plenty of fruit, especially apples, which are rich in potassium, pears, citrus fruit, unsprayed grapes, apricots, peaches and melons. Well-chewed pips and seeds, eaten in moderation are a good source of trace elements. Fresh or dried figs and bananas are highly nutritious. Unsulphured, sun-dried fruit — prunes, raisins, sultanas, figs, Hunza apricots — cooked in a little water and steeped overnight — make a nourishing breakfast dish. After three to six months, depending on your progress, you may add a few fresh nuts in their natural state, but not salted or roasted, to your food. They must be freshly shelled, since they go rancid quickly. AVOID peanuts and brazil nuts, which are too rich in oil.

16. Eat plenty of vegetables, including tomatoes, carrots, beetroot, cauliflower, celeriac, fresh beans and peas, leeks, green leaf vegetables, including lettuce, cos lettuce, Chinese cabbage, green peppers, aubergines, marrow, brussel sprouts and spinach. AVOID CELERY, CUCUMBER, PARSLEY AND PARSNIPS. These contain small quantities of carcinogens, which are damaging to the cancer patient, though safe

in small amounts for the healthy person. Dried pulses, e.g. brown lentils, beans and chick peas should be soaked overnight and allowed to start sprouting before cooking. Potatoes and sweet potatoes should be baked in their jackets, but consumption of the actual skins should be avoided. Eat as much garlic as you can bear, both raw and cooked, with your food; also onions.

17. Sprouting grains and seeds are living packages of valuable nutrients and enzymes. Sprouting alfalfa is an especially important source of zinc, of which most cancer patients are short, and which plays an important part in prostaglandin production. Soak alfalfa, brown lentils, mung and aduki beans or chick peas overnight in a glass jar, covered with cheesecloth secured with a rubber band. Drain carefully, and rinse well twice a day. Between rinses jars should lie on their sides in a warm place. The sprouts are ready when they have grown both root and shoot. Eat them before green leaves develop. If you can't, store the jars in the refrigerator to halt development. Also grow wheat grass in trays of moist peat, first soaking the organically grown wheat overnight. Cut the "grass" when it is 15 – 20 cms. long, chop finely, and add to soups, salads, vegetable stews. The grass can also be ground to produce a valuable nourishing juice, which can be diluted with a little water and drunk several times a day. If you want a breakfast cereal that is different, grind 2 – 3 tablespoonfuls of organic whole wheat; moisten with water and allow to stand overnight; in the morning add lemon juice and sliced or grated apple. Experiment with sprouting buckwheat, oats, barley and millet. The latter is especially valuable for cancer patients as a source of mandelonitriles.

18. Use UNBLENDED honey in small amounts instead of sugar for sweetening. (Blended varieties of honey have usually been subjected to heat in the blending process, and have lost much of their goodness.)

19. In the case of active disease 10 – 15 GRAMMES of additional vitamin C should be taken every day. This can be

obtained in tablets, and also in the form of a powder of calcium ascorbate which can be added to drinks. When the tablets are taken, these should be in the form of slow release tablets, to avoid flooding the body all at one time. The daily does should be divided into four equal doses and taken at equally spaced intervals over the twenty-four hours. Provided that sufficient liquid is taken during the day this dose is perfectly safe for cancer patients, though it may initially lead to loose motions in some people. It is best to work up to it gradually over period of about three weeks. Vitamin C has a dual role in cancer. Not only is it concerned with prostaglandin production, but also concerned in the metabolism of collagen, the essential constituent of fibrous tissue and cartilage, and it assists in the body's efforts to wall off and encapsulate the cancer so as to prevent it from spreading. This should be supplemented with daily doses of oil of evening primrose, 500 mgs. three times a day. Oil of evening primrose is the main source for the body of cislinoleic acid, which is the essential raw material for prostaglandin production.

DETOXIFICATION

Cleansing the organism of toxins is a most important part of all natural systems of cancer control. Toxins accumulate in the body for a number of reasons, including the death and destruction of cancer cells, and there are a number of different ways of removing them.

1. In some methods, particularly in the Gerson therapy, frequent coffee enemas are used to detoxify the body. Besides speeding up the elimination of toxic residues through the stimulation of the liver, they also bring about a remarkable reduction of pain within 2 – 3 days, and also bring quick relief from headaches, nausea, etc. To prepare, add three tablespoons of freshly ground, medium roasted Columbian coffee (NOT INSTANT COFFEE!!) to a litre of purified water. Boil for three minutes, then simmer for 15 minutes. Allow to cool and then strain into a measuring jug. If the

volume has been reduced in the cooking, add water to bring it up to a litre. Using a gravity fed enema kit (obtainable in England from John Bell & Croyden, Wigmore Street, London W1 or from your local chemist), administering the enema at blood heat while lying on your left side with your knees drawn up to your chest. Do not have the height of the reservoir more than 50 cms. above the body. Lubricate the end of the tube with a little KY Jelly before inserting and insert it GENTLY to a distance of about 8 – 10 cms. Allow the coffee to flow in slowly and endeavour to retain it for about 15 minutes in the colon before passing it. It is advisable, since this is a retention enema, that the bowels should have been evacuated shortly before the enema is given. Some people find it easier to administer the enema in two instalments, voiding the first before introducing the second and retaining each for 12 – 15 minutes. In severe and active cases the enema may be repeated at two hourly intervals with considerable benefit. More usually administration three times a day will be sufficient.

2. Medical opinion is divided on the subject of enemas. At the Bristol Cancer Help Centre a liquid extract of liver stimulating herbs is recommended instead to be taken by mouth to promote detoxification. This is held to avoid the possible overstimulation of the system by the absorption of caffeine from the enema. However, in cases where pain is a predominating feature, the coffee enema is still considered to be preferable. The extract of liver herbs can be ordered from Argyll Herbalists, Coombe Wood, Winscombe, Somerset BS25 1DG at a cost of about £6.50 per bottle. It is also available from Nature's Own Ltd., 203/205 West Malvern Road, West Malvern, Worcs., WR14 4BB.

3. Unless a cancer patient is very weak and underweight, a 48 or 72 hour fast can be undertaken on fresh vegetable and fruit juices and spring water. This is often a very useful introduction to the diet. It is important to have a complete rest during the fast, maintaining a calm and peaceful state of mind. Further brief fasts can be carried at monthly intervals while the cancer is active, or whenever the appetite flags.

4. Try to make your environment as chemical-free as possible. Discard sprays, make-up, hair-lacquer, hair dyes and perms, nail varnish, scented soaps, toothpaste containing fluoride, mothballs, insecticides and similar preparations. Use only Weleda non-toxic deodorant. If you are a gardener, discard all toxic chemicals. It is better to be over-careful than to add further toxins to an already overloaded body.

CONCLUSION

It is most important that diet should not become in itself yet a further source of stress to the patient. It must be pleasant and acceptable. What has been written above is to be regarded as the general principles of diet for the cancer patient. But because every patient is an individual, it is not possible to lay down a blanket, over-all prescription for diet which will be suitable for each and every patient. These general rules have to be tailored to suit each individual patient. Moreover the diet should not be attempted except under knowledgeable medical supervision, and then only in combination with a full mineral and vitamin programme, backed up by counselling, psychotherapy, meditation and visualisation exercises and regular healings. DIET BY ITSELF IS NOT SUFFICIENT TO ESTABLISH CONTROL OVER CANCER. THE NON-TOXIC APPROACH NEEDS TO BE FULLY HOLISTIC, and the full mineral and vitamin programme must be carefully designed to meet the needs of the individual patient.

CHAPTER 6

Some Guidelines on Forming and Running a Cancer Group

With the growing number of cancer support groups forming across the country, I am often asked for guidance in how to go about forming a group. There are a number of points which have to be considered. First and foremost it is important to have clearly in mind what is to be the nature of the help to be offered and the range of 'therapies' to be covered. Broadly speaking cancer groups fall into two classes: those which, like the Bristol Cancer Help Centre, offer a wide range of the complementary therapies, and which are competent to initiate a course of self-help for patients; and those which aim primarily at offering support to patients who have either already attended such a centre and embarked upon such a course, or those whose main needs are social, psychological and spiritual support, while undergoing orthodox therapies. Which class a group falls into is likely to be determined in the first place by the range of skills available to the group and the level of training and expertise of the personnel in running the group.

Groups of the first class, that is to say centres offering the full range of complementary therapies, need to be built around an experienced, trained and caring doctor, familiar both with nutritional and metabolic aspects of cancer therapy, and with techniques of psychotherapy, deep relaxation, meditation and imaging, and bio-feedback. He will see all patients attending the group prior to their first attendance, and subsequently at regular intervals (though not necessarily on each attendance) for the purpose of monitoring their progress. Together with the nutritionist he will help to establish a suitable nutritional programme for each patient, and will advise about the range and dosage of additional vitamins and minerals required, and whether additional aids to healing such as Iscador are indicated. He will keep the family doctor and the oncologist informed of these, and see that wherever possible they are supplied by the family doctor on NHS prescription. He will also review with the patient the course of orthodox therapy being offered, whether it be surgery, radiation therapy or chemotherapy, and advise the patient to what extent he/she should comply with the suggestions of the oncologist or surgeon. (In this respect it is important that the therapies being offered by the group should not be viewed as an alternative to normal therapy, but should be seen as complementing it. However, it will always be borne in mind that in the long run some levels of orthodox therapy may in the end be counterproductive.)

Following this, the patient will see the group leader, and be instructed in deep relaxation and meditation, together with imaging. At this point it may be helpful if the patient is given a tape to help in the practice of relaxation and imaging, but it must be made clear from the outset that listening to someone else meditating is not the same as doing it for oneself. The patient should also be seen as soon as possible by a psychotherapist/counsellor. Persons working in this field will need to have undergone some training in counselling, and will for preference be professionally qualified in this sphere. They will also need to have some special instruction in those aspects of phychotherapy relating to cancer. Since the relationship between therapist and patient needs to be founded upon a basis of mutual respect and liking, it is unlikely that the same psychotherapist will suit every patient. There will thus probably be a need for more than one psychotherapist at the centre. In any case it is important to see that the case load of each individual therapist does not become too heavy for them to handle. While group sessions can be of great value in the psychotherapy of cancer, it must be remembered that not all patients are comfortable in a group environment, and, in any case, psychotherapy sessions need to be conducted on a private, one-to-one basis.

Finally, the area of spiritual healing needs to be explored with the patient. The giving of spiritual healing is of the highest importance in cancer, but it must be remembered that not all patients, at least initially, are ready to accept this form of help. Many may have deep fears or religious prejudices over this, so that it is important that patients are not exposed to spiritual healing until they are ready to accept it. Many spiritual healers will come from a Spiritualist background, and it is of the very highest importance that no attempt is ever made to proselytise the patient. All spiritual healing, however mediated, is Divine in origin, and healers should remember to be on their guard against making reference to healing guides, discarnate helpers, karmic patterns and so on. Ill-timed remarks of this sort can often put a patient off and even drive him/her away from the group. Only when the patient has passed through all these initial stages is he/she ready to be introduced into the group sessions.

The size of the group sessions is of some importance. My personal experience has been that it is inadvisable to allow an individual group to grow too large. Twelve patients is probably the maximum for any group session, with seven being the ideal number. Thus it may well be necessary, when the centre is properly under way, to have a number of separate groups operating. The frequency for meetings is something that will be determined by the individual circumstances of the group. Ideally each patient with an active cancer should probably attend once a week, or failing this, at least fortnightly. Patients whose cancers are quiescent, or who have already attended for a year, may well only need to come at monthly intervals, provided that they are keeping up their meditation at home. Space should be made in the group for the attendance of members of the families of the patients, and wherever possible attempts should be made to involve the closest relative (child or spouse) in regular attendance at the group.

Some attention needs to be paid to the room in which the group works. An institutional environment is not the most suited for generating the energy patterns required in healing cancer. The colours of the decor should be soft pastel shades, with blue and gold predominant. Suitable curtains and pictures should be provided, and an effort made to have fresh flowers present at every group meditation. Lighting needs to be subdued, with either low wattage table lamps or candles being the preferable source. Fluorescent tubes are bad and should be avoided. The overall atmosphere should be one of serenity and tranquillity. Music is also of great value in creating the right atmosphere, and attempts should be made to build a library of suitable music for use in the group sessions and to provide a cassette machine for playing this.

Each group session should have the psychotherapist in attendance as well as the group leader and healers, since matters may sometimes surface in a group environment which need training and experience if they are to be rightly handled. It is also to be hoped that the doctor overseeing the centre will attend whenever possible. (This will benefit him personally, as well as the patients!) Thus the room in which the group meets needs to be of sufficient size to accommodate around 30 people, allowing for a full attendance of relatives, together with patients and healers, group leader, psychotherapist and doctor(s). A desirable patient healer ratio is 1:3(4). It may also be necessary to allow space for observers and occasional visitors.

The accommodation required by a full centre must therefore be able to contain individual rooms for use by the doctor, group leader, nutritionist and psychotherapists. Kitchen facilities are desirable, so that patients and relatives can receive training in the preparation of suitable foods and menus. Instruction includes instruction in juicing, sprouting, the making of yoghourt and of home-made bread and wholeflour baking. There will have to be space for a receptionist and telephonist and a waiting area for patients.

Groups of the second type will need less elaborate arrangements, and will often function round the home of a dedicated individual. Such groups will not aim at more than supportive therapy, with help in queries over diet, and group meetings for meditation and healing. Where skilled counsellors are available, this can be added to the facilities offered. The main function of these groups will be that of providing ongoing help in meditation and imaging, nutritional counselling and encouragement, and regular healing. Ideally they should be linked with centres of the first type, of which they may be regarded as an extension. They should also, wherever possible, be closely associated with hospital cancer clinics, with the intention of ensuring that patients are brought into contact with these supportive therapies right at the outset of their disease, and not left in the state of fear and outrage which so often follows a diagnonis of cancer. The personnel required will therefore be: a group leader, who should be familiar with the whole range of the holistic approach, a counsellor/psychotherapist, a nutritionist, and one or more healers. The same considerations apply as in the first group as to size of group, frequency of meeting and nature of meeting place.

Both types of group should endeavour to build up a library of instructional material, such as books and tapes and should try to have available for purchase a range of natural health foods and vitamins. (A local health food shop might well be willing to be associated with the group for this purpose.) They should also try to help patients in finding organically grown food, and should be familiar with local sources of supply.

Funding of groups will need to be done on a local basis. Healers and other personnel involved may well need to have travelling expenses covered, and there will need to be funds available to cover the cost of premises, heating, lighting and so on. Patients making use of the facilities will need to be educated to contribute, perhaps on a donation basis for this purpose. In the case of centres of the first type it may be necessary to charge a fee for each attendance. Professionally qualified psychotherapists and counsellors may also need to be remunerated for their work, perhaps on a sessional basis. The importance of patient contributions is twofold. Firstly it must be remembered that the whole basis of the holistic approach is one of self-help and the acceptance by the patient of responsibility for health care. The giving of a donation is an affirmation by the patient that this responsibility has been accepted. Secondly it is of the utmost importance that once a group has started it does not collapse from lack of the essential wherewithal to continue its work. Such a collapse, and the subsequent withdrawal of help, could be disastrous for many patients. Therefore before any group starts up, there must be adequate funds available, and once the decision has been taken to start a group, a concerted fund-raising drive is necessary. Subsequently other fund-raising drives such as jumble sales, coffee mornings, sponsored walks, and collecting boxes in shops, especially health food stores, must be organised on a regular basis. These will also have the effect of keeping the group before the public eye, and of maintaining local interest. In the case of full centres, operating on a fee-charging basis, consideration should be given to starting a bursary fund for those unable to afford the full charges.

The best way of starting a group is probably through the holding of one or more public meetings at which the holistic approach can be presented. (NAC can help with the provision of suitable speakers for such meetings.) If there is a sufficient degree of public support and interest, it should then be possible to set up a small working party to plan the formation of the group/centre. The working party which will probably have to meet a number of times, will be concerned with the acquisition of suitable premises (making certain that suitable parking facilities are available), the finding of the right personnel to run the group, and with arrangements for financing the group. The initiative for group formation should come from local sources. (Only so can the necessary enthusiasm for the continued running of the group be generated.) Patients and their relatives, healers, practitioners of 'alternative' therapies, social workers, nurses, and members of local community health councils are likely sources for help. Where a Natural Health Centre already exists, this may well form the nucleus for the new group. However, where this is so, it must be remembered that the problems of the cancer patient are of a very special nature, and that experience has shown that it is not satisfactory to mix cancer patients with patients suffering from other chronic diseases, such as multiple sclerosis, rheumatoid arthritis, hypertension etc. in the same group. Every effort should be made to secure the interest and support of local medical practitioners, but should this not be forthcoming, as in the present state of medical opinion it may well not be, this should not be considered a hindrance. Doctors may well start to become interested, when they can see how much patients are helped by attendance at the group.

It is also important to try to ensure that the group is not seen as a last resort for those for whom contemporary orthodox therapy has been unsuccessful, and that it is not seen as a form of terminal care. The whole emphasis of the holistic approach is upon healing, and not upon support, and patients should be encouraged to come right at the outset, even before conventional therapy has been commenced. Experience has shown that, when this is done, patients respond far better to orthodox therapy, and have a far better chance of complete recovery than when holistic therapy is delayed until orthodox therapy has been exhausted. The healing of cancer comes about when the patient has been through a process of personal transformation, and the aim of holistic therapy is to assist in bringing this about.

All persons associated with the running of the group should make every effort to educate themselves in the holistic approach through attendance at the various national seminars and workshops organised by NAC, and through a concentrated course of reading and study. The following list of books should be considered as suggested reading:

New Approaches to Cancer: Shirley Harrison: Century Hutchinson £6.95.
Getting Well Again: Carl and Stephanie Simonton: Bantam Books £1.50.
Mind as Healer, Mind as Slayer: Kenneth Pelletier, Allen & Unwin
You Can Fight For Your Life: Laurence LeShan, De Vorss, N.Y.
The Gate of Healing: Ian Pearce, Neville Spearman £7.50.
Bristol Programme: Penny Brohn: Century Hutchinson £4.95.
An End to Cancer: Leon Chaitow, Thorsons.

All these books can probably be obtained from Watkins Bookshop, 21 Cecil Court, Charing Cross Road, London.

New Centres and groups should affiliate to NAC, who should be kept fully in the picture. There is a constant stream of requests for help from cancer patients all over the country, so that it is important that NAC is kept informed of the facilities available, so as to know where to refer patients for help.

It is important that all groups should be completely ecumenical, and that any form of institutionalised religious bias be studiously avoided. If a group becomes identified with any particular religious or spiritual path, this can become a hindrance to its work, and present a barrier to some in need of help. Patients need to feel completely safe within their own personal religious guidelines. However, since the healing of cancer involves personal transformation on the part of the patient, and a major part of the work of the group is in assisting this process, there has to be a strong spiritual element in the group, whatever may be the pathway being followed by individuals. Workers in the groups must be able to be all things to all people, and will have to remember to keep their own religious and spiritual prejudices in the background. There must be no attempts at conversion. Each person finds their own pathway to God out of their own experiences in life. Our task is only to help and guide, and not attempt to pressurise people into following our pathway.

CHAPTER 7

Future Prevention

It is now proposed to turn from the therapy of active cancers to the direction in which our preventive approach should be moving in the years to come. One may perhaps draw an analogy from tuberculosis, once the great killer disease of western society, and attended a century and a half ago with all the horror attached to cancer today. Tuberculosis has now been practically eradicated as a major cause of death in the west. Initially the emphasis was upon therapy, with isolation of patients in sanatoria, and the use of radical surgery and chemotherapeutic drugs as the main methods employed. It was not until it was realised that this was primarily a disease of poor housing and social conditions, and measures were taken to eliminate these, to identify the susceptible, and thus remove the reservoir of infection, and to raise the general level of resistance through the BCG campaign, that the disease was finally conquered. (The eradication of bovine tuberculosis also, of course, played an important part in the process.) We need to draw a lesson from this in our approach to cancer.

Our first task must obviously be to address ourselves to those patients who are actually suffering from cancer. We MUST introduce into our therapeutic regimes measures to help them overcome their lowered immunity. This means carefully structured psychotherapeutic programmes designed to reinforce and restore depleted immune systems, and the avoidance of all forms of therapy liable to damage them still further. As has already been hinted, one of the reasons for the appalling track record in the treatment of breast cancer is the massive psychological trauma inflicted upon the patient by radical surgery. Any process as mutilating as mastectomy seems to her to be an essential attack upon her femininity and to threaten in all sorts of ways her life, both inner and outer. Incredible as it may seem, a patient of the writer's was actually advised to have a second mastectomy in order to prevent a possible development of the cancer in her remaining breast! Such a lack of sensitivity seems difficult to condone, in the light of the knowledge that there are other methods of approaching the problem, Such a procedure MUST threaten still further an already depleted immune system. Another area to be considered very carefully must be the use of steroids in the treatment of cancer. These are already known to have a depressing influence upon the immune-rejection mechanism, and are already used for that purpose in transplant surgery. It is also extremely probable that one of the ways in which stress operates to depress the immune system is through the stimulation of the steroid production of the body. Cytotoxic drugs are also profoundly depressing to the white cell count, and should be reviewed very carefully to see whether the ultimate balance resulting from their use is on the credit or debit side of the account. Too often, one feels, they are employed to satisfy the need of the physician to be doing something, without sufficient weight being given to the degree of advantage to be obtained from their use. A further area which should be looked at more thoroughly is whether it may not be possible to stimulate the immune system by well-planned metabolic programmes. BCG is already being used for this purpose by a number of oncologists for certain types of cancer.

It is not proposed to enter here into the controversy over the use of Laetrile (amygdalin), save to say that this requires to be looked at afresh, without any preconceived ideas, using an active form of the chemical, and free from the lobbying of vested interests, whether professional or commercial. The last trial, carried out by the F.D.A. of America, left a good deal to be desired as far as the methodology of the trial was concerned. In particular, future trials should be combined with correct nutrition, and adequate records should be kept of the amount of chemotherapy and radiation which the patients have received beforehand. In particular, some patients in the early stages of cancer should be included, who have not been subjected to immuno-destructive therapy. The results now being obtained by Nieper, at the Silbernsee Clinic, Hanover and by Contreras at Tijuana in Mexico, suggest that the whole story has been far from told.

From the preventive aspect we need to educate the public at large in the importance of correct eating and the avoidance of foods contaminated with artificial chemicals, both in production and in processing. In this respect the food, farming and horticultural industries are far from blameless. The public must also learn to understand the crucial importance to the prevention of disease of maintaining right attitudes and mental outlooks. Since so many of these stem from interpersonal relationships between parents and children, and between brothers and sisters, this process needs to be begun in the nursery, and in the mother and child clinics. A better understanding of these factors by general practitioners and health visitors would enable them to help parents to form such relationships, and to avoid the unhappy state of affairs related in some of the case histories quoted. There is need, too, for a far greater appreciation of the skills of psychotherapists, and a far wider use made of their skills and training. Every primary care team should include a psychotherapist, whose role should be regarded at least as much from the preventive as from the therapeutic point of view. The training of health visitors in elementary psychotherapy, and especially in the link between family relationships and subsequent cancer development, would also be advantageous, and enable them to play a wider role in helping people to remain healthy and in balance.

Finally, the supreme importance of inculcating correct eating habits cannot be overstressed. Reference has already been made to the importance of this from the therapeutic point of view. It is not without significance that cancer is a relatively rare disease among many primitive societies.

As long as 1913 Albert Schweitzer came to the conclusion that the remarkable freedom from cancer of the people of Gabon must be related to dietetic factors. In his preface to Alexander Bergals' *Cancer: Cause and Cure*, (Pasteur Inst.

Paris, 1957) He wrote:

> On my arrival in Gabon in 1913 I was astonished to encounter no cases of cancer. I saw none among the natives two hundred miles from the coast . . . I cannot, of course, say positively that there was no cancer at all, but like other frontier doctors, I can only say that if any cases existed, they must have been quite rare. This absence of cancer seemed to be due to the difference in nutrition of the natives as compared with the Europeans.

A further significant observation was made by Dr Moerman of the Netherlands. Following the occupation of the Netherlands by Nazi Germany in 1940 a drastic change in dietary habits took place. White bread disappeared completely and was replaced by wholemeal bread and rye bread. The supply of sugar was greatly reduced, and the import of oil for margarine was stopped. The population were forced to rely far more upon fruit and vegetables to satisfy their hunger, and meat became virtually unobtainable. Following the end of the occupation and of this enforced austerity and people reverted to their normal feeding habits: white bread, milk, much sugar, much meat, few vegetables, and relatively little fruit. The result of this enforced change was that the official cancer rate published by the Netherlands Department of Welfare and Health dropped from a peak in 1942 to its lowest-ever level in 1945. Since 1945, with the resumption of a diet containing large amounts of meat and processed foods, it began to climb again, and has remained at its previous high rate ever since.

Other interesting evidence comes from the work of Sir Robert McCarrison among the inhabitants of the remote kingdom of Hunza in the Himalayas. These people are renowned for their longevity, and for the fact that visiting medical teams from the West report that there has never been a case of cancer in Hunza. McCarrison, writing in the Journal of the American Medical Association (Jan 7, 1922) reported:

> The Hunza has no known incidence of cancer . . . They have an abundant crop of apricots. These they dry in the sun, and use very largely in their food.

In 1973, Prince Mohammed Khan, son of the Mir of Hunza, told Charles Hillinger of the *Los Angeles Times* that the average expectation of life of his people is about 85 years. "Many members" he added, of the Council of Elders, "who help my father govern the State, have been over 100." (*Los Angeles Times*, May 7, 1973.) It was not unusual, said the Prince, for people to eat 30 to 50 apricot seeds as an after-lunch snack. (The significance of this for us is that the apricot kernel is a rich source of the contraversal amygdalin, otherwise known as laetrile, referred to in appendix D in technical details.) In addition to the apricot, which forms a staple part of their diet the Hunzas' diet consists largely of grain and fresh vegetables including buckwheat, millet, alfalfa, peas, broad beans, turnips, lettuce, sprouting pulse and berries of various sorts.

In 1927 McCarrison was appointed Director of Nutrition Research in India. He experimented with the effect of the Hunza diet upon albino rats to see what the effect would be compared to the diet of western countries. In a series of over 1,000 rats, observed from birth up to the age of 27 months, at which point the rats were killed and autopsied, McCarrison reported:

> "During the past two and a half years there has been no case of illness in the *universe* of albino rats, no death from natural causes, and apart from a few accidental deaths, no infantile mortality. Both clinically, and at post-mortem examination of this stock it has been shown to be remarkably free from disease. It may be that some of them have cryptic disease of one kind or another, but, if so, I have failed to find either clinical or microscopic evidence of it."
>
> Renee Taylor, *Hunza Health Secrets*: Award Books, New York, 1964.

In follow-up experiments, McCarrison fed the rats on typical Indian and Pakistani diets, when they soon developed eye ailments, ulcers, boils, bad teeth, crooked spines, loss of hair, anaemia, heart, kidney and glandular disorders. In yet a further series of experiments the rats were fed on a diet of white bread, margarine, sweetened tea, boiled vegetables, canned meat and cheap jams and jellies, a diet not dissimilar to that of many families today. The rats responded by developing all sorts of metabolic disorders, and showing various types of unnatural behaviour patterns. McCarrison reported:

> "They were nervous and apt to bite their attendants; they lived unhappily, and by the sixteenth day of the experiment, they began to kill and eat the weaker ones among them."

There are numerous other societies which have been found to be remarkably free of cancer. The Hopi and Navajo Indians of Arizona have an incidence of cancer that remains remarkably low. In 1949, the Journal of the American Medical Association declared:

> "The Indians' diet seemed to be remarkably low in quality and quantity, and wanting in variety, and the doctors wondered if this had anything to do with the fact that only 36 cases of malignant cancer were found out of 36,000 admissions to the Ganado Mission Hospital. In the same population of white people, the doctors said, there would have been about 1,800."

The Eskimo are another society who have been found to be totally free of cancer. The Eskimo diet is rich in meat from animals grazing upon the Tundra grass, and on the salmon berry, which grows in profusion in Arctic areas. They also eat as a particular delicacy, a green salad made from the partly digested stomach contents of caribou and reindeer, which have been grazing on the Tundra. When the Eskimo abandon their traditional way of life and move into settlements where they feed upon a western style diet, they are even more prone to cancer than the average white man. It has been suggested by some that the crucial factor in the Eskimo diet is the high nitriloside content of the Tundra grass. (The nitrilosides are chemically closely related to amygdalin.)

Many other primitive peoples also show the same pattern of freedom from cancer, and longevity. Notable among these are the Abkhasians, from the Caucasus mountains, whose health records rival that of the Hunzas.

It may of course be argued that such people are not subjected to the levels of stress and pollution experienced by those living in western style democracies. Were they to breathe the same smog-filled air, smoke the same cigarettes, swallow the same chemicals added to their food and drinking water, use the same soaps and deodorants, then their incidence of cancer would be similar. This is a valid argument. But if we look at the incidence of cancer in such groups as the Seventh Day Adventists, who live mainly in California, and of the Mormons, who live in Utah, we find a similarly low cancer rate. Among the Seventh Day Adventists the cancer incidence is less than 50 per cent of that of the rest of the population of California. (The reason that their rate is still high compared to some other communities in other lands is probably that many of these are converts who have not always adhered to a vegetarian diet.) Similarly, among the Mormons, the rate is 25 per cent lower for men and 38 per cent lower for woman than in the rest of Utah. The fundamental difference between these two groups and the rest of the population is that both are strict vegetarian, non-smoking and teetotal groups.

Professor Sir Richard Doll and Dr Richard Peto, in their important paper submitted to the United States Congress on the level of environmental cancer risks, came to the conclusion that in the United States no less than 35 per cent of cancer deaths were attributable to diet. Their figures showed striking correlations between certain types of cancer and feeding habits. For example, in New Zealand and the United States, where the average daily intake of meat amounts to 320 and 280 grammes, respectively, the respective deaths from cancer of the colon amounted to 45 and 33 per 100,000 population. At the other end of the scale, in Nigeria and Japan, where the average daily meat intake is less than 40 grammes per day, deaths from cancer of the colon amount to only 2 and 5 per 100,000 population respectively. A similar relationship between animal fat consumption and breast cancer can be shown, with the Netherlands and Denmark topping the scale with 150 grammes per day total fat intake and a death of 25 per 100,000 population.

The inference for our approach to cancer to be drawn from

these observations is distressingly obvious. Maybe we ARE digging our graves with our teeth!

All of these, of course, are long term measures. Most are considered heretical by medical thought. But a new approach in professional thinking is long overdue. We can no longer take refuge from the figures in a rigidly mechanistic, technological approach. *Cancer must be seen for what it is, not a disease in its own right, but an indicator of underlying biological inadequacies and attention directed towards the processes through which these are brought about.* The views expressed here are condemned as heresy by most of the profession, and those who propagate them as quacks and charlatans. But the history of all advances in knowledge has run the same course. Galileo was nearly burnt at the stake for expressing views that are regarded as commonplace today. Lister and Simpson were ridiculed for their concepts on antisepsis and anaesthesia. Pasteur fought long and hard before his ideas of bacteria were accepted. Moerman was vilified in his own country, and Semmelweiss was crucified in Vienna for suggesting that midwives should wash their hands. But so often history has shown that the heresy of today becomes the orthodoxy of tomorrow. The writer is content to leave this to the judgement of history. What is needed, above all else, is minds to be kept fresh and open, ever ready to try out new ideas and to consider new methods; not casting out entirely the old ways, but amplifying and extending them by grafting on to the best of the old the inspiration of the new.

Avoiding Cancer

Most cancers could be avoided if the individual had known sufficiently how to do so. This appendix sets out protective measures which all can take. Cancer arises in several different ways:

(a) Occasional errors in the process or cell renewal in all our bodies may damage a healthy cell and cause it to mutate. Gamma radiation, asbestos dust, tobacco smoke, diesel fumes and many others are known to be cancer producing.

(b) An upsetting emotional shock or a series of distressing events may result in the release of steroid hormones into the blood stream with consequent suppression of the immune system, and thus the capacity to resist cancer. This is more likely to occur in the case of those whose personalities are ill adapted to handling changes in life and in relating to others.

(c) Free radical cells in the blood stream resulting from the exposure to certain liquids and chemicals can cause mutations of healthy cells.

(d) In a few cases there may be inherited deficiency in the immume system.

Where abnormal cells arise, the heathy body attacks and destroys them through the activity of the T-lymphocytes and other protector cells of the immune system. If, however, the immune system is working inefficiently through lack of ultra-violet light in the eyes, or lack of Vitamin C or A, or because of excessive steroid production through stress, the cells can multiply unchecked and form a tumour. Also if the body tissues are in a state of anoxia (oxygen starvation) due to a high fat diet, or a deficiency in potassium, the cancer cells are encouraged to proliferate, since they do not require oxygen. Similarly those people whose tissues are well oxygenated, because they eat little fat or oil are better able to resist cancer cell proliferation, because their oxygen rich tissues inhibit cancer cell growth.

TO AVOID CANCER TAKE THE FOLLOWING STEPS:

1) Adopt a cheerful contented lifestyle, free from excessive emotional stress. Practice a system of deep relaxation every day and learn to take life — and people — as they come. Take time to consider your own essential needs in life and ensure that they are met. Learn to forgive — yourself and all others who need it — and to express love in your daily life towards all whom you meet. Allow an hour every day to do something which gives you joy and pleasure and cultivate a sense of fun so that you laugh often.

2) Try to avoid as much as possible exposure to known carcinogens in the environment. These include excessive levels of nitrates in foodstuffs; tobacco smoke (especially when combined with alcohol consumption); over consumption of red meat (leads to bowel stasis and the development of bacteria producing carcinogenic exotoxins within the bowel); hydrocarbons in foodstuffs resulting from heating of fats and oils; toxic dusts such as asbestos, hard woods, leather dusts; radiation; minerals such as chromium and nickel; coal tar and its derivatives; pesticides and insecticides; smoked meats and fish, which often contain amounts of creosote and formaldehyde; high levels of coffee intake (roasting of coffee beans produces matrol, which is carcinogenic); fumes from incomplete combustion in central heating boilers; some industrial solvents as used in paint and aerosol sprays. Fluoride is believed by many to have a carcinogenic influence, although

the evidence here is still not complete. Excessive exposure to sunlight may also trigger off cancers in susceptible people.

3) Whenever possible eat organically grown, unsprayed fruit, vegetables and grains. EAT THE FOODS WHEN THEY ARE VERY FRESH. Avoid overcooking and pressure cooking. Pressure cooking does not materially affect the vitamin content of foods but it does seriously diminish the enzyme content. Meat should be from poultry or animals reared on unsprayed land free of artificial fertilisers, and the animal should be free of hormone and antibiotic injections. Eat not more than two eggs a week because of the high cholesterol content of egg yolks. Avoid all foods which contain added salt, sugar, flavourings, preservatives, dyes, and other chemical additives.

4) Take at least half an hour every day for exercise appropriate to your physical condition. Swimming is excellent; jogging rather less so.

5) Do not wear sunglasses unless you have to do so. Ultraviolet light acting directly on the eyes promotes vitamin A formation which is protective against cancer.

6) Use only stainless steel or enamel or Pyrex cooking utensils; not aluminium or non-stick.

7) Use bicarbonate of soda for washing up and rinse thoroughly under a hot running tap.

8) Use only bland, unscented soaps and shampoos.

9) Electricity is best for heating and cooking. Where gas, calor gas, oil or paraffin must be used be careful to see that there is a proper extraction system for gases resulting from incomplete combustion.

10) Filter tap water before drinking or cooking in it, and whenever possible try to use spring water which is low in salt.

PROTECTIVE FOOD SUPPLEMENTS

Vitamin A	one teaspoonful cod liver oil daily, or one Halibut or Cod Liver Oil capsule.
Vitamin B	three tablets Brewers Yeast daily, or one B Complex tablet.
Vitamin C	1 – 2 grammes daily combined with bioflavonoids.
Vitamin E	400 i.u. daily (except in breast, uterine and ovarian cancers.
Selenium	200 micrograms daily.
Iodine	300 mgm. Kelp tablets, 2 daily.

PROTECTIVE FOODS

These foods strengthen the body's immume system and discourage cell proliferation:
All vegetables and fruits (especially the following):

Apples and pips	Alfalfa	Aubergine
Asparagus	Brussels Sprouts	Beetroot
Cabbage	Carrots	Cauliflower
Chicory	Comfrey	Chives
Cassava	Chinese leaves	Dandelion
French Beans	Garlic	Kale
Leek	Lettuce	Onions
Pears and pips	Peppers (green only)	Potatoes
Pumpkin	Runner beans	Radish
Seaweed	Spinach	Sweet potatoes
Tomatoes	Turnips	Watercress
Yams	Pulses	Fresh fruits
Sun dried fruits	Juices (vegetable &	Herb teas
Herbs	fruit no sugar)	Grapes (especially

All forms of sprouted seeds, grains, beans and whole, unprocessed cereals.

N.B. PARSNIPS, CELERY AND PARSLEY TO BE AVOIDED. They contain psoralens, which are carcinogenic.

FOODS CONTAINING VITAMIN B17

The following foods are rich in B17, an anticarcinogenic agent, and you should try to include them in your diet.

Alfalfa	Apple pips	Beet top
Spinach	Linseed	Apricot kernels
Sweet potatoes	Pear pips	Peach kernels
Watercress	Yams	Plum kernels
Lentils	Lima beans	Nectarine kernels
Cranberries	Mung beans	Prune kernels
Elderberries	Green peas	Currants
Gooseberries	Blackeye beans	Chick peas
Mulberries	Almonds	Cashew nuts
Guavas	Buckwheat millett	

N.B. Beans need to be soaked for twelve hours before careful cooking. See Appendix E for details of preparation.

(Author's Note. I am indebted to my friend and colleague, David Holmes FRSH, MIHE, Dip.Ed., of New Approaches to Cancer and of the Wessex Cancer Help Centre, for much of the information in this appendix.)

Diet: Some Technical Considerations

The success of the immune systems in dealing with cancerous cells seems to be dependent on the correct functioning of the T-lymphocytes, or T-cells. These cells, which form part of the white corpuscles of the blood, appear to be controlled by the level of Prostaglandin E1 present in the body. This is formed in the body via dihomogammalinoleic acid and gammalinoleic acid from the essential fatty acid, linoleic acid. This is partly stored within the body and partly ingested in the food. The process of conversion into Prostaglandin E1 is inhibited by carbohydrates. certain fatty foods, ageing, insulin lack, opiates, the products of partial digestion of wheat and other cereals, and alpha-casein (the main protein in dairy products). It is reinforced by Vitamin B6 (pyridoxine) — growth — and vitamin C. The mobilisation of linoleic acid from the body stores is inhibited by carbohydrates. Moreover, there are two forms of linoleic acid, known as the cis- and the trans- form, according to the arrangement of the atoms within the molecule. Of these only the cis- form is able to be transformed into gammalinoleic acid. Up to 40 per cent of that present in hydrogenated oils is in the trans- form, as are most of the polyunsaturated fatty acids in the diet. The cis- forms are only available from vegetables. Moreover, they are not very common at that. Worse still, not only are the trans- forms useless for prostaglandin production, but they actually block the conversion of the cis- form into gamma-linoleic acid. The next step in the biochemical chain, the transformation of gammalinoleic acid into dihomogamma-linoleic acid takes place without much difficulty, but most of that formed becomes incorporated in the membrane stores of the body. For the mobilisation of this, zinc is necessary. Cancer patients, however, are in a state of zinc deficiency, resulting from the challenge to the host by the tumour cells producing a state of zinc depletion. Thus additional zinc requires to be administered. For the final step, that of transformation of dihomogammalinoleic acid into Prostaglandin E1, Vitamin C is necessary. However, unless there is enough dihomogammalinoleic acid free in the body — i.e. not locked up in the membrane stores — it is useless to take additional Vitamin C. For the efficient utilisation of Vitamin C the presence of a sufficiency of zinc is essential. Thus it may well be that much of our susceptibility to cancer may be massively reinforced by our own dietary deficiencies.

Dietary Supplements

Revised for this edition to take account of recent advances in clinical practice, by Dr. Peter Mansfield, M.A., M.B., B.Chir., a friend and colleague of the late author.

Vitamin A: stimulates the thymus gland source of T-lymphocytes and assists in the de-shielding of cancer cells.

It is best given in the form of Emulsified Beta-Carotene, which the body turns into Vitamin A according to need. This can be obtained in capsule form and dosages up to 50,000 International Units per day are suggested, but do not exceed the dosage which just begins to stain the palms of the hands yellow.

Other signs of possible excess dosage are HEADACHE (due to fluid retention in the brain); MYASTHENIA (muscle weakness): HAEMORRHAGE from nose, throat etc. **If any of these three signs occur, Beta Carotene should be immediately stopped.**

Vitamin B1: Can be taken in the form of tablets, 6 – 10 mg daily, (three tablets twice a day) + brewer's yeast (3 tablets three times a day). One high potency Vitamin B Complex can be taken instead of Brewer's Yeast, if preferred.

Vitamin C: Is efficient in activating the suprarenals and thus increasing the production of tumosterone. For this purpose take 4 – 6 grammes daily, in the form of 500 mg slow release tablets, in 3 – 4 doses daily. However Pauling, Cameron and others claim that in sufficiently high doses Vitamin C has a destructive effect upon the cancer cell, and there is a good deal of evidence to substantiate this view. For this purpose, doses of up to 20 – 25 grammes a day need to be taken. As the body acts as a sort of weir, with a body level at which any excess of Vitamin C is rapidly excreted, this needs to be given in carefully spaced doses at four to six hourly intervals, spread evenly through the 24 hours. For this purpose, it is essential that a non-acid form be used, such as Calcium Ascorbate plus Bioflavonoids.

Vitamin D: Is the precursor of thymosterone and tumosterone. This is essential, and can be given in the form of calcium orotate with 250 i.u. Vitamin D2, one tablet twice daily.

Vitamin E: THIS IS TO BE AVOIDED IN HORMONE-SENSITIVE TUMOURS — e.g. IN BREAST CANCER.

SODIUM: IS TO BE AVOIDED IN ALL PATIENTS WITH CANCER i.e. NO SALT!! Its role in the body is to control potassium balance. In the cancer patient this is best achieved by giving magnesium, which can be taken in all cases in the form of magnesium orotate, 500 mg twice daily. Alternatively use Dolomite 500 mg tablets which is a mixture containing 240 mg calcium carbonate and 200 mg magnesium carbonate; but you will need 500 mg of Vitamin C (preferably as Calcium Ascorbate) with each tablet to be sure of absorbing it.

Zinc: Care has to be taken with the administration of zinc. Although this is vitally necessary for prostaglandin production in which role it acts in conjunction with vitamin C, excess of zinc could precipitate cardiac problems in patients predisposed in that direction. Except in the case of lymphoma, where much larger doses can be given, dosage of zinc should not exceed 100 mg daily of zinc orotate. Some cheeses, such as cottage cheese and crowdie, actually interfere with zinc metabolism, and are to be avoided.

Calcium: Is especially important in bone cancer, where it should be taken in the form of calcium orotate to a level of two grammes daily. In other than bone cancers, this can be combined with magnesium in the form of dolomite.

Selenium: Is an essential activator of certain enzymes involved in the immune system. It is becoming depleted in the soil through general soil exhaustion. This is particularly so in certain geographical areas. A dose of 500 mcg (microgrammes) daily should be taken in all cases.

Copper: Is a counter-acting element against zinc. Copper is excreted by the cell system as the tumour develops and grows in size, thus leading to a rise in blood copper levels, and a corresponding fall in blood zinc levels. (This forms a convenient way of monitoring tumour activity by comparison of levels at different stages of therapy.) It has been shown in Germany that **small** doses of copper in the form of 100 mcg (100 microgrammes or 0.1 milligrammes) restores the deficiency of copper in cancer patients' body cells and decreases tumour activity.

Germanium: Promotes oxygen function and reduces free radicals. This is best taken as a peptide-bound complex which is readily absorbed and retained by the body. A dose of 15 mg elemental Germanium in this form is recommended daily.

Some Recipes and Menus

The author is indebted to The Bristol Cancer Help Centre for much of the information contained within this section.

A WEEKLY MENU

MONDAY

Breakfast:	Muesli with sesame seeds, buckwheat, wheatgerm, fresh peaches, apple juice
	Slices of wholemeal bread
	Banana and tahini spread
	Peppermint tea
Mid-morning:	Sliced apple
	Fresh fruit juice or herb tea
Lunch:	Fresh carrot juice
	Beetroot, courgette, lettuce, mung bean sprouts and carrot salad
	Wholemeal bread
	Orange and banana surprise
Mid afternoon:	Wholemeal bread with apple & almond spread
	Rose hip tea
Dinner:	Savoury brown rice with chopped nuts
	Mixed salad or carrot, cauliflower, onion, radish
	Wholemeal bread
	Spinach soup
	Mixed fresh fruit salad

Before bed: Glass of fresh apple juice

TUESDAY

Breakfast:
: Cooked buckwheat, millet, barley cereal with fresh orange juice
  Slices of wholemeal bread
  Apple and nut spread
  Camomile tea

Mid-morning:
: Banana
  Fresh carrot juice

Lunch:
: Mixed bean sprouts, courgette and lettuce salad
  Wholemeal bread
  Lentil and onion soup
  Apple and grapefruit (fresh) cocktail

Mid-afternoon:
: Banana and tahini spread on wholemeal bread
  Peppermint tea

Dinner:
: Apple and carrot juice
  Mixed lettuce, alfalfa sprout salad with fresh herbs
  Baked jacket potato
  Fresh grapes

Before bed:
: Cup of rosemary tea

WEDNESDAY

Breakfast:
: Muesli with a little goat's milk yoghourt and fresh pears and grapes
  Slices of wholemeal bread
  Fresh sage and lemon tea

Mid-morning:
: Apple juice

Lunch:
: Raw salad of lettuce, cabbage, chopped hazel nuts, sprouts, beetroot leaves, chives and mint

Brown bread
Onion and carrot soup sprinkled with
    brewer's yeast

Mid-afternoon: Slice of wholemeal bread with banana
    and orange spread
Rose hip tea

Dinner: Large helping of brown rice salad, grated
    beetroot, chopped nuts and onion salad
Apple and wheatgerm surprise

Before bed: Elderflower tea with ½ tsp honey

THURSDAY

Breakfast: Cooked cereal with fresh orange and
    grapefruit
Wholemeal bread with apple, almond and
    tahini spread
Mint tea

Mid-morning: Fresh fruit juice or herb tea
Apple (raw)

Lunch: Green salad
Leek and potato soup
Wholemeal bread
Fresh fruit

Mid-afternoon: Camomile tea
Banana

Dinner: Apple juice
Large portion of coleslaw
Cooked brown rice, with herbs, onion
    and nuts
Baked apple with raisins

Before bed: Lemon and thyme tea

FRIDAY

Breakfast: Muesli with a little goat's milk yoghourt
    and fresh orange and apple

	Wholemeal bread
	Peppermint tea
Mid-morning:	Fresh carrot and orange juice
	Apple (raw)
Lunch:	Red cabbage and orange salad, with chopped nuts
	Spiced vegetable soup with brewer's yeast
	Wholemeal bread
Mid-afternoon:	Raspberry and yoghourt fool
	Rose hip tea
	Pear (raw)
Dinner:	Onion, lettuce and fresh herb salad
	Wholewheat bread
	Mixed bean stew or casserole
	Apple mousse
Before bed:	Lemon balm tea

SATURDAY

Breakfast:	Cooked cereal with fresh pears and grapes
	Wholemeal bread with banana and orange spread
	Rose hip tea
Mid-morning:	Fresh carrot and apple juice
Lunch:	Large portion green salad with chopped nuts
	Creamed onion soup
	Wholemeal bread
	Apple and yoghourt fool
Mid-afternoon:	Camomile tea
	Banana
Dinner:	Fresh beetroot and lemon juice
	Brown rice pilaff
	Large portion Spanish salad with sprouted seeds
	Apple and wheatgerm surprise

Before bed: Rosemary tea

SUNDAY

Breakfast: Muesli with soaked dried apricots and
                    apple juice
                Wholemeal bread with a little honey (½
                    tsp)
                Mint tea
Mid-morning: Fresh carrot and apple juice
Lunch: Baked vegetable casserole with tahini and
                    coriander sauce
                Large portion of green salad and whole-
                    meal bread
                Watercress (or lettuce) soup with whole-
                    meal bread
                Fresh fruit
Mid-afternoon: Rose hip tea
Dinner: Fresh carrot, parsley and apple juice
                Winter-borsch with wholemeal bread
                Dandelion salad with humus
                Orange and banana surprise
Before bed: Peppermint tea

MUESLI

Do not buy ready mixed muesli, which usually contains
added sugar and milk powder. Buy an organically grown
muesli base, and add to this buckwheat, sesame seeds,
sunflower seeds wheat germ (keep it in the fridge), raisins,
currants and any other convenient dried fruits. Soak this
overnight (you can use fresh apple juice for this if you like).
Before serving add as many different kinds of nuts as you
can, together with fresh fruit in season. A little yoghourt can
be added, or soya milk. If sweetening is required, use a little
honey.

COOKED CEREAL

Soak overnight:

½ tbs whole buckwheat	½ tbs whole millet
½ tbs flaked oats	½ tbs flaked wheat, barley or rye

Simmer over low heat until desired consistency (5 – 10 mins). Eat with fresh fruit and a little yoghourt.

Tahini and Banana Spread

Mash up one banana with a tablespoonful of tahini. Put into blender, adding lemon juice and one tablespoonful of sunflower seed oil. Blend until smooth and use as a spread on wholemeal bread or toast. If liked, a few chopped almonds or teaspoonsful of buckwheat may be added to give a crunchy taste.

Apple and Almond Spread

Chop apple and put into liquidizer with a few almonds and raisins. Blend until smooth, add a little tahini to bind and a teaspoonful of safflower oil and lemon juice to taste.

SALADS

Coleslaw

½ lb hard cabbage	1 med carrot
1 med apple	1 med onion

Shred the above together finely and dress with the following:

1 dessertspoonful oil	1 sprig of borage or
2 tsps lemon juice	parsley chopped
2 comfrey leaves (chopped)	

lemon juice or yoghourt dressing may be added to taste.

Red Cabbage and Orange Salad

Peel and cut into small pieces ½ orange and juice from other half. Chop ½ lb red cabbage finely, add some chives, parsley and the rest of the orange, mix well with the orange pieces and dress with the juice.

Sprouted Alfalfa Salad

2 tbs sprouted alfalfa   1 med carrot, grated
1 tspn chopped chives   ½ bunch watercress,
        chopped
Mix together and dress with a little lemon and oil dressing.

Dandelion Salad

1 good handful of young   ½ bunch watercress,
  and tender dandelion   chopped
  leaves   1 tbsp parsley, chopped
few spring onions chives,
  chopped
Mix together and serve with lemon and oil dressing.

Spanish Salad

1 onion thinly sliced   1 orange in slices and
some finely chopped   chopped
  chicory   a little shredded lettuce
1 tsp chopped mint
Mix together, with a dressing if preferred, and serve on lettuce leaves.

Sweet Potato Salad

1 lb sweet potatoes, boil and chop into squares — or slice while still warm, pour over the following dressing:

2 tsp oil   1 tbs lemon juice (or
1 med onion, finely   cider vinegar)
  chopped   1 clove garlic, crushed
Mix well with sweet potatoes and cool; serve sprinkled with
parsley or lemon balm.

Winter Salad

lettuce, chopped   apple, chopped
1 med carrot, grated   ½ beetroot, grated
Mix together with a dressing and serve on lettuce leaves with
chopped watercress.

Fennel Salad

1 good sized fennel bulb   1 large eating apple or
                              orange
Wash, slice and mix together. Dress with a little lemon juice
and serve on a bed of shredded cabbage or spinach leaves.

Stuffed Pear Salad

½ ripe dessert pear   ½ avocado pear
little lemon juice   little ginger
2 tsp sunflower seeds
Brush pear with lemon juice. Mash avocado with lemon
juice, ginger and sunflower seeds, and decorate with a few
grapes

Carrot and Orange Salad

Grate 2 carrots   Peel and chop 1 orange
Mix together with a little of the zest of the orange and 2 – 3
dessertspoons of orange juice. Try adding a little onion.

Beetroot and Apple Salad

Grate finely 1 beetroot and 1 apple. Add a little cumin or caraway seed (soaked for an hour in warm water) for extra flavour. Or try adding a little grated onion and carrot — also grated horseradish or ginger — if liked.

Fresh Spinach Salad

Wash and chop 1 handful spinach leaves; peel and chop 1 orange; chop 1 dessertspoonful almonds. Mix together with a little yoghourt, sprinkled with dill (dried in winter, fresh in spring).

Green Salad

Use all of these if possible, or as available:

lettuce, spinach cabbage	chives or spring onion
sprouts, beetroot leaves	chickweed (grows as a
watercress	weed in most gardens!)
mustard and cress, mint	parsley, comfrey leaves
borage, lemon balm	a little onion

Chop or shred together and mix with a little vinegar and oil dressing, yoghurt dressing, or orange juice for a change.

Asparagus — the Turkish Way

Cut asparagus into bite size pieces and boil in a little water until soft. Drain (keep the water to use in soup or drinks). While still warm arrange in dish and pour over Yoghourt Dressing No. 1, garnish with chopped dill, chives or both.

Yoghourt Dressing

1) Mix together

1 tbs yoghourt
1 onion finely chopped
a little crushed garlic
1 tspn lemon juice
½ tsp paprika

2) Liquidise or mix together:

1 tbs yoghourt
1 clove garlic crushed
½ tsp tarragon
fresh, or if dried, soaked
in lemon juice for 1 hour

Lemon and Oil Dressing

1 tbs lemon juice

2 tspn safflower, or sun-flower seed oil (all cold pressed)

SOUPS

Spinach Soup

Make a roux with 2 teaspoonfuls oil, 1 dessertspoon wholemeal flour, and add enough water or vegetable stock to make a soup consistency. Chop spinach leaves and cook in the sauce for 3 – 5 minutes, take off heat and put through liquidiser. (This can be done with all vegetables, including watercress, lettuce, onion and cauliflower, if you chop it into small pieces before cooking.)

Lentil and Onion Soup

3 oz lentils
¾ pint water
1 tsp oil
1 carrot

1 med onion chopped or in rings
1 bayleaf, some cloves
chopped chives or parsley

Wash lentils and cook in water and oil for approx. 10 minutes; then add chopped vegetables and stir these in. Bring to the boil and simmer gently until all is cooked, adding more water if necessary. Add a little lemon juice, and serve sprinkled with parsley or chives. Liquidise, if preferred smooth.

Onion and Carrot Soup

1 large onion	2 med carrots
a little cooked (if any over)	

Chop vegetables and cook in water until tender. Liquidise and add a little milk (if allowed). Serve sprinkled with chopped parsley and brewers' yeast.

Leek and Potato Soup

2 large leeks, washed and chopped	1 med. potato (WITH SKIN) scrubbed and
some ground nuts	chopped into cubes

Chop vegetables, boil in water until soft, and liquidise, adding a little lemon juice or cider vinegar to taste. Serve sprinkled with brewers' years and chopped chives.

Baked Sweet Potatoes

These are a different vegetable from our ordinary potatoes. They are best baked in their skins like ordinary potatoes. Serve with a vegetable casserole, or with salad, dressed with a yoghourt dressing.

Leek and Artichoke Soup

1 leek (chopped)	1 bayleaf
3 artichokes (chopped)	1 clove of garlic
2 carrots (chopped)	a little basil

Add 1 pint of vegetable stock and cook until soft. Liquidise and serve sprinkled with a little dill.

Spiced Vegetable Soup

1 med onion	1 parsnip
2 med carrots	1 turnip or swede
1 leek	a little cabbage

Chop and cook in a little water until soft, adding 1 tsp each of aniseed, marjoram and dill. Either liquidise or eat as a 'hot-pot' type of soup. Serve sprinkled with brewers' yeast and/or seaweed or parsley.

Baked Vegetable Casserole with Tahini and Coriander Sauce

1 med onion chopped
1 parsnip chopped
1 leek

1 carrot chopped
some Jerusalem artichokes

Put together in a casserole with a little water and bake in oven until tender. Make a white sauce with wholemeal flour and oil. Add liquid from casserole, a little lemon juice and 1 level tbs tahini and ½ tsp coriander. Pour over casserole and serve hot.

Vegetable Casserole

1 med carrot chopped
2 dessertspoons brown
  lentils
1 dessertspoon oatflakes
  (for thickening)

1 med parsnip chopped
1 onion chopped
1 tsp each of sage and
  thyme
½ cooking apple chopped

Cover with water or vegetable stock, and bake in oven in a tight lidded casserole until tender.

Roast Vegetable Casserole

Scrub well and chop the following vegetables:
Sweet potato, leek, carrot, artichoke, onion (peeled)
Parboil and place in ready oiled oven dish; saute some garlic in a little oil and pour over vegetables. Roast in oven until tender. Serve with lentil sauce.

Lentil Sauce

Cook a quantity of green lentils with some carrots, onions, turnip and garlic. When soft, puree in liquidiser, adding dill, basil and sage (or mint). Thicken with wholemeal flour if necessary.

Creamed Onion Soup

8 oz chopped onion	1 dessertspoon oil
1 tbs wholemeal flour	1 pint water or stock

Boil onion in stock until tender; heat oil in saucepan and add flour, stirring in the onion and water. Add more water if too thick. Liquidise, and serve sprinkled with brewers' yeast and chopped parsley.

Winter Borsch

1 dessertspoon oil	1 onion
1 large beetroot grated	1 carrot grated
1 red cabbage chopped	

Lightly saute all the vegetables and then add water to cover. Simmer until all the vegetables are tender; add ½ cup tomato juice, chopped fresh (or dried) dill, and parsley. Serve sprinkled with brewers' yeast and a little yoghourt.

Summerfruit Soup

¼ lb strawberries or other soft fruit	½ pint strong vegetable stock

Liquidise and simmer for 1 – 2 minutes. Cool and blend in 1 tbs yoghourt and serve with chopped mint or lemon balm, or chives.

CASSEROLES ETC.

Walnut and Mushroom Casserole

2 – 3 oz halved walnuts	mixed herbs
2 – 3 oz mushrooms	a little vecon or vegetable

1 large carrot, sliced in rings
1 dessertspon oil or spring water

seasoning
1 heaped tbs flaked oats
1 large onion chopped

Saute onions and carrot in oil before adding to rest of ingredients. Cover with water, adding 1 tsp. vecon and mixed herbs. Cover with tight fitting lid and cook in oven until tender.

Bean and Wheat Casserole

3 oz black eyed beans
3 oz adzuki beans
3 large onion slices
2 tbs cracked wheat

washed well and soaked overnight

1 clove garlic

1 bay leaf or other seasoning (marjoram, dill, sage etc.)

Cover all ingredients with vegetable stock and cook in tightly lidded casserole for one hour, or until tender. Just before serving add crushed garlic and ½ tspn vecon. Raisins or sultanas can be added if liked.

RICE

Brown rice should always be used in place of white. This is because it still has the outer skin, which contains useful amounts of vitamin B, iron and calcium, which white rice lacks. It takes a little longer to cook, but has a pleasant nutty taste.

Savoury Brown Rice

1 cup brown rice
1 cup boiling water
1 large onion
2 oz mushrooms

1 tsp oil
1 tsp mixed herbs or fresh sage
1 tbs chopped cucmuber

Wash rice well, bring water to boil, add oil, rice and other chopped vegetables. Bring to boil, and simmer gently with lid closed for 30 minutes. Sunflower seeds, raisins and dill seeds may be added for variety.

Rice Salad

Boil one cup of rice in 1 cut of water, with 1 bay leaf and a little rosemary. When cooked, cool, and dress with a little oil, cider vinegar. Add chopped fresh parsley, chives or raw onion (chopped) and dried apricots (soaked and chopped).

Rice with Herbs

Instead of cooking the rice with all the herbs, try boiling it with the bay leaf, and adding fresh chopped rosemary, sage, chives, lemon balm and parsley after cooking, when it has cooled. Dress with a little cider vinegar and oil and garlic dressing.

Rice Pilaff

a cup of rice
1 leek
1 med onion, chopped

1 oz sultanas or chopped apricots

Boil water (1 – 1 ¼ cups) until tender. Serve dressed with 1 tsp oil. Sprinkle with whole almonds (not skinned) and a little banana if liked.

Macaroni and Cashew Nut Cheese

½ cup cashew nuts
2 oz red pepper
3 tbs lemon juice
3 tbs brewers' yeast
1 cup whole wheat macaroni

1 grated onion
Speck of garlic power or crushed garlic
½ tsp vecon
1 tbs oil

Crumbs Topping
½ cup whole wheat crumbs
tbs brewers' yeast

combine

Cook macaroni for 15 min; add 1 tbs oil and mix lightly. While macaroni is cooking combine cheese mix in blender until very fine. Add to macaroni and put in casserole. Bake 30 min with cover on. Sprinkle with crumb topping and bake uncovered for further 15 min.

NUTS AND BEANS

When you are not eating meat, you rely upon the pulses (beans), nuts, seeds and yoghourt for your protein needs. You must eat as great a variety of these as you can manage to ensure that your diet is properly balanced and that all the necessary amino acids are contained in it. There are many different varieties of beans, most of which need separate treatment in preparation — e.g. soaking, cooking times etc. So it is important to understand a little about bean cookery. A valuable source of information and recipes is *The Bean Book* by Rose Elliott, published in paperback by Fontana. Among the different varieties of bean are the following:

Adzuki Beans: small and reddish brown, with a strong nutty flavour, and much used in the macrobiotic diet. Imported from the Orient, where they are usually cooked to a soft consistency and served with coconut milk or rice.

Black Beans: one of the kidney bean family, they are large, black and shiny. Like all the kidney beans they cook to a soft and succulent texture, and are useful in casseroles and salads when mixed with other beans. They can be substituted for red kidney beans in any of the recipes.

Black Eyed Beans: smaller than black beans, creamy coloured and kidney shaped, with a distinctive black spot or eye. One of the quicker cooking pulses, with a pleasant savoury flavour and succulent texture, they can be used as a substitute for haricot or butter beans.

Butter Beans: probably the best known bean in England. They are large, flat, kidney shaped and creamy white. They need careful cooking so as to be tender but not end up as a mush.

Haricot Beans: small and oval in shape, and creamy white in colour. Best known in England in the form of 'baked beans', but can be used in many ways.

Mung Beans: best known in their sprouted form, in the form of bean shoots. Small, rounded and green in colour, they are one of the quicker cooking beans and can be cooked without soaking.

Red Kidney Beans: rich red in colour and kidney shaped, they cook to a delicious mealy texture. They are excellent both in salads and more substantial dishes.

Soya Beans: have the highest protein content of any of the pulses. They are small, round and yellowish-brown in colour. They are the hardest of the beans and need prolonged soaking followed by several hours cooking and careful seasoning. They are also the source of soya flour, which is useful for enriching the protein value of other foods. It can also be used to make non-dairy milk (soya-milk), and two types of 'cheese'. One of these, known as 'bean curd' is widely used in Chinese cookery, and can usually be bought from shops selling Chinese foods.

Chick Peas: light golden brown in colour, and the size of hazel nuts. Particularly appetising flavour when cooked.

Green Lentils: may be grey, green or even reddish brown in colour. Useful in cooking in that they retain their shape after cooking, unlike red lentils.

Red Lentils: freely available in supermarkets! Unlike most pulses they do not need to be soaked before cooking. They cook to a soft mass, and have a pleasant, bland flavour.

Pulses are reputed to be 'very windy foods'. The secret seems to lie in correct preparation. Some of the saccharides contained in pulses, such as raffinose, stachyose and verbascose, may not be reduced in the small intestine to metabolisable sugars, and thus enter the large intestine, where they are digested by the bacteria present, with the production of gases such as carbon dioxide, methane and hydrogen, which cause flatulence. Most people, however, contain within the large intestine bacteria capable of converting the saccharides into non-gaseous metabolites. The secret of digestion would appear, however, to be closely connected with the preparation of the beans. If you have trouble digesting them, it would be worth while taking extra care in their preparation, and perhaps concentrating on the thinner-skinned varieties. The thinner skinned they are, the quicker they cook.

Preparation and Cooking

Washing: rinse thoroughly in a bowl of cold water to get rid of all dust, and then finally, in a large sieve.

Soaking: 1) Long cold soak: cover with twice their volume of cold water and leave for 4 – 8 hours to soak, or overnight.
    2) Short hot soak: put the washed pulses into a saucepan, cover with plenty of cold water, and bring to the boil. Allow to boil vigorously for 3 – 4 minutes, then remove from heat, cover the saucepan and leave to soak for 45 – 60 minutes.

Rinsing: after soaking, put the pulses into a large sieve and rinse thoroughly under cold running water. If you have difficulty in digesting them, follow this by further parboiling-and-rinsing; put the pulses into a saucepan, cover with cold water and boil for 5 minutes. Then turn out into a colander and rinse again with cold running water.

Cooking

Put the pulses into a saucepan or casserole and cover with plenty of cold water or stock. DO NOT ADD SALT — IT TOUGHENS THE OUTSIDE OF THE BEANS AND PREVENTS PROPER COOKING. Acid juices, such as lemon juice and tomatoes, have a similar effect and should be added after the initial cooking. Slow cooking, at the bottom of the oven is particularly appropriate.

Cooking Times

Adzuki beans	30 minutes
Black beans	1 hour
Black eyed beans	30 – 40 minutes

Barlotti beans		1 hour
British field beans		30 minutes
Broad beans		1½ hours
Butter beans		1¼ hours
Cannellini beans		1 hour
Chick peas		1 – 1½ hours
Continental lentils green	soaked	30 – 40 minutes
	unsoaked	1 – 1¼ hours
Haricot beans		1 – 1½ hours
Kidney beans		1 hour
Mung beans	soaked	20 – 30 minutes
	unsoaked	30 – 40 minutes
Peas		45 minutes
Red split lentils	soaked	15 – 20 minutes
	unsoaked	20 – 30 minutes
Soya beans		3 – 4 hours
Split peas	soaked	30 minutes
	unsoaked	40 – 45 minutes

SPROUTING BEANS

Sprouting beans are a particularly valuable way of combining the protein value of the beans with providing a rich source of vitamin C and active enzymes. Kirlian photographs of the sprouting beans also show that they are very rich in the vital energy of living food. Basically 'sprouting' means keeping the beans damp and warm for a period of 3 – 6 days until they start to shoot. A handful of bean sprouts mixed with salad or thrown into soups and casseroles not only greatly increases its food value, but provides a delightfully crisp textured, crunchy addition to the dish. While the easiest and classic beans to sprout are the little green mung beans, any other good quality beans or dried peas may be used in the same way. Chick peas are especially good, as are adzuki beans and whole lentils.

The Method: remember that the beans increase greatly in volume during the sprouting process, so do not overfill the jar. Wash the beans, cover with cold water, and leave to soak overnight. Next day pour off the water and put the beans in a large, clean jar, and cover the mouth of the jar with a piece of muslin. Put the jar in the airing cupboard or other warm, dark place. Each day rinse the beans through with lukewarm water, and replace in the airing cupboard after carefully draining off the water. (Certain toxic substances are given off by the bean skins during the process, which must be carefully rinsed away. Hence the reason for rinsing every day.) After a day or two the beans will commence to sprout. Keep on rinsing and keeping in the dark and use when the sprouts are about one inch long.

When the sprouts are ready, turn out of the jar into a bowl of fresh cold water and swill around thoroughly. Then drain and use as required.

YOGHOURT

Yoghourt is a very valuable addition to the cancer patient's diet. It is also very useful in many vegetarian dishes. It is best made from goats' milk, if you can get it. It should be smooth and creamy, and firm enough to cut with a spoon. Here is how to make it.

1 pint milk	2 rounded tbs skimmed
1 tsp fresh, natural	milk powder
yoghourt or saved from	
previous batch	

Put milk into a saucepan, bring to boil, and allow to simmer for 10 minutes. (This reduces the milk a little, and helps to make the yoghourt nice and thick.) Then take the saucepan off the heat and allow to cool to blood heat. Add the skimmed milk powder and yoghourt and beat into milk with an egg whisk. Then place into a sterilised container jar, cover with foil, and place in a warm place to set. (This will take from 12 – 18 hours, depending on the temprature and the activity of the yoghourt added.) When set, put into refrigerator until ready for use. It is possible to buy thermostatically controlled apparatus for making yoghourt, which can be useful if you have problems over the temperature, but this should not be necessary.

To sterilise your jars, swill them out with hot water to which has been added a teaspoon of household bleach, or some sterilising powder such as is sold for wine making. Rinse with warm water very thoroughly afterwards. (Sterilise the egg whisk too!)

Some Recipes with Beans

Aigrossade

8 oz potatoes	1 or more large cloves
4 oz new carrots	garlic crushed
4 oz shelled broad beans	6 tbs mayonnaise
4 oz French beans	6 tbs natural yoghourt
14 oz artichoke hearts	chopped parsley and
4 oz chick peas, soaked,	chives
cooked and rinsed	

Scrape potatoes and carrots and cook in boiling water until nearly tender. Wash shelled broad beans, top and tail French beans and add to pan of pototoes and carrots. When all the vegetables are tender, drain and cool them and cut into even-sized pieces. Drain and slice artichoke hearts and mix with other vegetables, together with the chick peas. Mix together the mayonnaise and yoghourt, then add the vegetables, turning them so that all are coated with the mayonnaise mixture. Sprinkle with chopped parsley and chives and serve with warm wholewheat rolls.

Bean Sprout and Cabbage Salad

12 oz hard white	1 tbs cold pressed oil
cabbage	lemon juice
3 large pears, peeled and	8 oz bean sprouts
cut into chunks	

Wash and finely shred the cabbage and put into large bowl. Wash and drain the bean sprouts. Add the bean sprouts and pear to the cabbage, together with the oil, a very little finely ground black pepper and lemon juice to taste.

Bean Curd, Sultana and Carrot Salad

6 oz bean curd	1 tspn soy sauce
2 large carrots	2 tbs orange juice
4 oz sultanas	1 tbs cold pressed oil
½ tsp sugar	½tsp dried mustard

Cut bean curd into small squares; scrape and coarsely grate carrots. Wash sultanas, and put into small bowl and cover with boiling water; leave 10 – 15 minutes to plump up, and then drain. Beat together in a small bowl the orange juice, oil, sugar, mustard and soy sauce. Put the curd squares, carrots and sultanas into a bowl, pour over the dressing and turn salad gently with a spoon until everything is coated. Be careful not to break up the bean curd. Serve sprinkled with chopped chives.

This salad is especially rich in protein and can form a main course.

Bean Salad

4 oz beans soaked and cooked until tender then drained	2 tbs fresh chopped green herbs
2 large carrots, scraped and coarsely grated	1 green pepper, deseeded and sliced
1 apple diced	4 inch cucumber, diced
2 tbs cider vinegar	6 tbs cold pressed oil
1 tsp sugar	½ tsp dry mustard

Put the oil, mustard, vinegar and sugar into a salad bowl with a little black pepper. Stir to blend everything and then add the beans, green herbs, and the rest of the ingredients. Mix well so that everything is coated with the dressing and serve with wholemeal bread.

Chick Pea Salad

6 oz chick peas	1 small onion, peeled and
2 cloves garlic	sliced into rings

2 tbs oil	2 tbs lemon juice
freshly ground black pepper	3 tbs chopped parsley

Cover the chick peas with water and leave overnight. Then drain and rinse thoroughly with cold water. Cook until tender in fresh cold water, then rinse and drain thoroughly. Peel and crush garlic and put into medium sized bowl together with oil, lemon juice and black pepper. Add the drained chick peas and turn them in the dressing. Add onion and parsley and leave to get cold. Serve chilled.

Chick Pea and Spinach Salad

1 lb spinach	6 oz chick peas, cooked
6 tbs oil	and drained
2 tbs cider vinegar	¼ pin natural yoghourt
2 tbs chopped parsley	black pepper

Wash the spinach thoroughly and cook without extra water until tender. Then cool, drain and chop it. Add the chick peas to the cooled spinach, along with the oil, vinegar and black pepper. Mix well, and chill until required. To serve arrange spinach and chick pea mixture on a plate; spoon over the yoghourt, and sprinkled with chopped parsley. Serve with wholemeal bread. A few onion rings will add a crunchy texture to the salad mixture.

Humus

4 oz cooked chick peas	1 – cloves garlic
2 tbs lemon juice	4 tbs cold pressed oil
2 tbs tahini (sesame cream from health food shops)	

Soak, rinse and drain the chick peas, and then cook until tender and drain, reserving the cooking water. Put chick peas into liquidiser goblet, together with 4 – 5 tbs of cooking water, garlic, lemon juice, tahini and half the olive oil, and liquidise until smooth, adding more water if necessary. Chill the mixture. To serve, spoon on to a flat dish, smooth and

then fork over the top before pouring remaining olive oil.
Sprinkle with paprika and garnish with lemon wedges.

This can be served as an addition to salad dishes or as a
spread on wholemeal bread, or as a 'starter'.

Rice and Bean Salad

4 oz red kidney beans	8 oz aubergine
8 oz long grain (or brown) rice	1 red pepper
	8 oz tomatoes
4 oz mushrooms	1 large onion
1 clove garlic	2 tbs oil
¾ pint water	freshly ground black
2 drops tabasco	pepper

Soak the beans, cook until tender and then drain. Wash the
rice, and put into saucepan with the water, bring to the boil
and cook very gently with the lid on until tender and all the
water has been absorbed (about 60 minutes with brown rice).

Wash the aubergine and cut into small pieces; sprinkle with
sea salt to draw out any bitter juices, then squeeze and rinse
the aubergine and dry in a cloth. Crush the garlic, peel and
chop the onion and fry together in the oil in a large saucepan
for 10 minutes. Add the aubergine and cook for a couple of
minutes while you de-seed and chop the pepper and slice the
mushrooms. Then add the pepper, mushrooms and sliced
tomatoes to the saucepan and cook for a further 10 minutes.

Mix together the cooked rice, vegetables and beans and
season with freshly ground black pepper and tabasco. Allow
to get quite cold and serve sprinkled with parsley.

Bean Bake

6 oz black eyed beans	2 large onions, peeled and sliced
1 clove garlic	
thyme	a little oil
½ pint vegetable stock	marjoram
2 tbs brewers' yeast	

Saute onions and garlic; add beans, herbs and vegetable stock.
Simmer gently until tender. Liquidise. Spoon into pie dish.

Top with wholewheat bread crumbs mixed with brewers' yeast, and bake until crisp on top.

A variation on this could be to rinse, soak and cook the beans before adding to onions and herbs, and to omit the liquidising.

Boston Baked Beans

12 oz haricot beans	2 tbs tomato puree
1 large onion	2 tsp brown sugar
1 tsp dry mustard	½ pint unsalted stock
2 tsp black treacle	½ pint tomato juice

Soak drain and rinse beans, and then cook until almost tender; then drain again. Set oven the 275°F (mark 1). Peel and slice onion. Heat oil in flameproof casserole and fry onion for about 5 minutes; then add rest of ingredients and bring mixture to boil. Cover casserole and put into oven; cook for about 4 hours with an occasional stir. (If preferred, you can use 4 oz fresh tomatoes and liquidise in blender.) Serve with hot wholemeal bread or wholemeal garlic bread.

Haricot Bean and Vegetable Pie

6 oz haricot beans	a little brown sugar
2 oz butter	1½ lb potatoes peeled
1 large onion, peeled and chopped	1 lb carrots, scraped and diced
1 large clove garlic, crushed	1 lb leeks, cleaned and sliced
¾ pink vegetable stock	a little milk
2 tbs tomato puree	½ tsp dried basil
freshly ground black pepper	4 oz grated cheese

Soak beans, then drain and rinse. Melt two-thirds of the butter in saucepan and fry onions for about 10 minutes, then add the drained beans, garlic and stock. Bring to the boil and simmer gently for about 1 hour until beans are soft and liquid reduced to a thick sauce. Stir in tomato puree, and season with basil, freshly ground black pepper and a little sugar if necessary. Meanwhile cook potatoes, carrots and leeks. Preheat oven to 375°F (mark 5), mash the potatoes using remaining butter and a drop of milk.

Grease shallow ovenproof casserole dish; put leeks and carrots in base; pour bean mixture on top; sprinkle most of the grated cheese, and then add potato topping. Fork over the potato and sprinkle with remaining grated cheese. Bake for 13 – 40 minutes, until crispy, golden brown on top, and serve with a green vegetable.

Bean and Grain Casserole

Use any kind of dried beans and/or peas, or lentils, and any kind of whole grain — i.e. brown rice, pot-barley, rye, buckwheat, millet, wheat — and soak overnight.

4 oz grain	4 oz beans
4 oz apricots	2 large onions, chopped
2 tbs oil	vegetable stock
1 large clove garlic, crushed	herbs to flavour generously

Sautee onion in oil in two saucepans, add soaked cereal to one pan, beans to other and cover with stock. Cover with close fitting lids and simmer on top of stove or in oven for appropriate time for cooking. (This will vary according to the beans used.) Stock should mostly be absorbed. Towards end of cooking time flavour generously with herbs (dill, basil, oregano or bay) and add garlic.

Split Pea Chowder

6 cups water	1 tbs brewers' yeast
½ cup brown rice	a little oil
2 cups split peas	½ cup finely diced carrots
1 cup sauteed onions	1 tsp basil
½ tsp coriander	½ tsp cumin

Add rice to rapidly boiling water and cook for 30 minutes; add split peas and cook for another 30 minutes; add onions, carrots and celery and basil and cook for another 15 minutes. Stir in brewers' yeast, coriander and cumin. Season with a little Ruthmol at the table.

Millet Rissoles

4 cups cooked millet   1 cup uncooked millet
½ cup ground almonds   2 large onions chopped
1 tbs cold pressed oil   1 tsp Vecon
2 bay leaves   celery seed, rosemary and
                      thyme to taste

Cover millet and bay leaves with 3 cups of water and simmer until all the water is absorbed. Sautee onion, and add with all other ingredients. Mix well and allow to cool. When cool, roll into balls and flatten into rissoles. Brush a stainless steel pan with a trace of oil, and bake to a golden brown.

Pie Crust

½ cup sesame seeds   ½ cup sunflower seeds
1 cup whole oats   1 cup wheatgerm
1 tsp kelp powder   ½ cup finely chopped
1½ tbs safflower oil   dates
1½ tbs water

Grind seeds and oats to powder in blender, and add oil and water whipped together to form an emulsion. Mix to a doughy consistency. Press into flat pie dishes and bake to golden brown. When cold, fill with fresh fruit. If liked, the filled dish can be lightly baked in the oven to form an Austrian torte.

Legal Cream

Core but do not peel two golden delicious apples; cube and blend with just enough apple juice to start blender. Add 1 tsp lemon juice. When purged, add 1 cup ground cashew nuts and continue to blend to a smooth cream.

Fruit and Yoghourt Fool

Use any variety of fresh fruit, or soaked dried apricots. Grate or mash and add 2 tbs yoghourt. Liquidise in blender. Serve sprinkled with chopped almonds, walnuts, brasil nuts aor sesame seeds. Fresh raspberries, blackberries, peaches, apples, bananas or oranges go extremely well in this recipe.

Orange and Banana Surprise

Liquidise 1 orange and 1 banana with a little lemon juice and serve sprinkled with a few sultanas and sesame seeds.

Postscript

Having read and hopefully digested the contents of this book, it is most important that the reader should be under no misapprehensions as to the scope and purpose of the Holistic Approach. Under NO circumstances can it be regarded as an alternative to orthodox therapy. It is NOT a way of avoiding those aspects of orthodox therapy to which the patient has taken a dislike, or of which he/she is afraid. While there are undoubtedly some aspects of normal therapy which need to be toned down or even eliminated, much of it is valid and of crucial importance to recovery.

The Holistic Approach, as has been already stated, depends upon recognising the different levels of body, emotions, mind and spirit upon which we all exist, and of the fact that each of these levels perpetually influences all the other levels. Only very rarely does a disease condition exist upon only one level. Therefore the therapy of that disease must be given at each level simultaneously. Thus it is impossible to pick and choose between diet, counselling and psychotherapy, meditation, and spiritual reorientation. All are important, and are in inverse order of as they recede from the purely physical plane. Moreover they COMPLEMENT orthodox therapy by taking therapy into areas and levels not reached by conventional methods, and, very often, as the attached letter from a patient shows, modifying the response to those methods. Let cancer sufferers start to attack their disease on all fronts, and at all levels of their being, recognising that their true healing comes from within themselves.

A LETTER FROM A PATIENT

"March 13, 1985.

Dear Dr. Pearce,

Last August I came to see you because I had cervical cancer. It is such a long time since I contacted you that if you thought of me at all, you must have assumed that I had died! Not at all! I am in perfect health, thanks in large measure to your advice and help. My cancer was stage 2B — the tumour had spread, but not very far. I had caesium implants (3), followed by four weeks of deep X-ray treatment, which made my guts very sore, so I couldn't follow your diet, but had to eat white, bland 'pap'. But I took all the vitamins, was helped by a healer, and did the visualisation meditation every day. The result was that though I lost weight, I gradually felt better during the treatment, not worse as the doctor expected. The only bad consequence was diarrhoea, and sensitive skin on my backside where the X-rays came out. When it was over, my doctor warned me that it could be several weeks before I would be back to normal food, and that I would suffer some pain. BUT — after ten days I was entirely normal (and walked nine miles round Greenham Common Air Base) and have never at any time suffered any pain!

The caesium implants destroyed my ovaries (I was not told of this, which made me furious) and I dreaded the immediate menopause. However I found out that oestrogen is made not only in the ovaries, but by other parts of the body too. So I did visualisation mediation about this, picturing oestrogen flowing through my body, bathing every part of it. I also took Ginseng. None of my fears materialised! Apart from one or two hot flushes every day, and no menstruation, I am fit, healthy, and just as I was before. So I feel I owe you a great deal.

The doctor was very surprised that I did so well. I tried to tell him what I was doing to help myself, but unfortunately he was not at all keen to hear about it. During the first week after coming back from the X-ray treatment I fasted two days on water to rest my sore insides, and then ate Slippery Elm bark with goats' milk, very gradually resuming my normal diet, so that by the end of ten days I was eating real brown bread, fruit, vegetables and beans. I never eat meat now, eat all whole food without additives, continue with Ginseng, and have never felt better in my life.

Thank you for what you did for me. How lucky I am to have met you and been given your advice.
Yours Sincerely
S.I."

I think that this letter shows very clearly the way in which the Holistic Approach combines with orthodox therapy. The following extract from another letter shows transformation in action.

". . . I was so pleased to hear from your wife last evening that you are doing well, and that everything is going to be O.K. (I have recently been undergoing surgery in hospital and am awaiting further treatment presently) I have thought about you a lot and have prayed for you.

I am keeping well and enjoying life. I am really getting on well with my new doctor. We have a good relationship — he is one of 'us'. I am having regular healing with Peter C. . ., whom I find is a really nice person.

I am still doing lots of swimming and walking and play badminton when I can. I am working hard with my music, both practical and theory; I love it so much. I have 2 exams soon, in May and June.

I am still keeping to the diet; I couldn't give it up now, I love it too much. I have 'invented' some wonderful recipes over the past couple of years; who knows I may even write a book one day!

I am doing my meditation etc. daily and enjoying it and am very happy . . .
With Love,
S."

The full story of S's cancer is told in the chapter "Working with the Holistic Approach". This letter, which is just one of many similar received, brings the story up to date.

Notes

Line	Page	Reference
7	22	Holmes, T. H. & Rahe, R. H.: The social readjustment rating scale. Journal of Pyschosomatic Research, 1967, 11, 213 – 18.
21	25	Thomas, C. B. & Duszynski, D. R.: Closeness to parents and the family constellation in a prospective study of five disease states: Suicide, mental illnes, malignant tumour, hypertension and coronary heart disease. The Johns Hopkins Medical Journal 1973, 134, 251 – 70.
1	26	Kissen, D. M.: Lung cancer, inhalation and personality: In Psychosomatic aspects of neoplastic disease. Philadelphia, Lippincott, 1963, 3 – 11.
		Kissen, D. M.: Personality factors in males conducive to lung cancer. British Journal of Medical Psychology, 1963, 36, 27.
9	26	Schmale, A. H. & Iker, H.: The psychological setting of uterine cancer. Annals of the New York Academy of Science, 1966, 125, 807 – 13.
16	26	Schmale, A. H. & Iker, H.: Hopelessness as a predictor of cercival cancer. Social Science and Medicine, 1971, 5, 91 – 100.
19	26	Greene, W. A.: Psychologiclal factors and reticuloendothelial disease: I. Preliminary observations on a group of males with lymphomas and leukaemia. Psychosomatic Medicine, 1954, 16, 22 – 30.
		—— The psychosocial setting of the development of leukaemia and lymphoma. Annals of the

146

New York Academy of Sciences, 1966, 125, 794 – 801.

Greene, W. A. & Young, L.: Psychological factors and reticuloendothelial disease: II. Observations on a group of women with lymphomas and leukaemia. Psychosomatic Medicine, 1956, 18, 284 – 303.

6   34   Greer, S. & Morris, T.: Psychological attributes of breast cancer: a controlled study. Journal of Psychosomatic Research, 1975, 19, 147 – 53.

7   34   immunoglobulin alpha. (A blood protein which has been found to vary in level with immune activity.)

6   36   linoleic acid: vide Horrabin, D. F. Journal of Holistic Medcine, 1981, 3; 2:119 – 139.
—— World Medicine, March 1981.

11   36   See above reference. Refined carbohydrates interfere with the prostaglandin chain, as does alpha-casein, the principle protein in dairy products.

14   36   The value of alcohol is partly a question of quantity, $(C_2H_5OH—>sugar)$ and partly a question of the nature of the alcohol. Light, dry wines are acceptable. Spirits, fortified wines and wines which are high in sugar content are not. ("Blood level 18% should read, "Blood level 18 mg %")

21   36   Bromelain: available in tablet form from "Nature's Own, 203/205 West Malvern Road, West Malvern, Worcestershire, England". Dose: one tablet mid morning and mid evening, between meals.

4   37   Vis Medicatrix Naturae: The healing power of nature — so referred to by the ancients.

10   44   Alpha rhythm: 8 – 12 Hz.

22   44   I have myself raised the skin temperature of my hands from 60 – 95°F. If takes much practice and training to achieve this unilaterally, but it is easy with both hands.

14   46   Smith, Justa: Enzymes are activated by the

laying on of hands. Human Dimensions, Vol. 1, No. 2. Miller, R. N.: Paraelectricity, a primary energy.

16   46   Grad, B.: Some biological effects of the laying on of hands; a review of experiments with animals and plants. Journal of American Society for Psychical Research, Vol. 59, no. 2, April 1965.

—— The "Laying on of Hands": Implications for psychotherapy, gentling, and the placebo effect. Ibid. Vol. 61, no. 4, Oct. 1967.

3   90   Iscador: Mistletoe, It has been widely used for the treatment of cancer in Europe for many years.

3   113   Vitamin C: One cannot generalise, as the dose must be carefully matched to the person and the level of disease present. As a general guide line, my current practice is to give 2 grammes twice a day prophylatically, or to patients with healed or inactive cancers, and 10 – 15 grammes daily to patients with active cancers. Doses as high as 20 – 25 grammes daily should only be used under supervision by a doctor experienced in their use. For further information see Cameron and Pauling's book, Cancer and Vitamin C: pub. 1979, The Linus Pauling Institute of Science and Medicine.

5   114   Crowdie: A kind of cottage cheese popular in Scotland and the north of England.

In addition to the books listed in Chapter 6, which must be considered as MANDATORY READING for all involved in cancer therapy, the following list is suggested for those who wish to undertake further study of the holistic approach. It must be understood that the author of *The Holistic Approach* does not necessarily endorse all the views and procedures recommended in these books.

Holistic Medicine: Kenneth Pelletier. Dela Corte Press, N.Y.

Cancer and Vitamin C: Cameron and Pauling. Warner Books, N.Y.

Cancer Therapy: Results of 50 Cases: Gersson. Totality Books, Del Mar, California

The Relaxation Response: Herbert Benson. Avon Books, N.Y.

Be Your Own Doctor: Ann Wigmore. Avery Publishing Group, Wayne, N.J.

Metabolic Ecology: Fred Rohe. Wedgstone Press, P.O. Box 175, Winfield, KS 67156, U.S.A.

The Clairvoyant Reality: Laurence Le Shan, Sphere Books, 30/ 32 Grays Inn Road, London.

The Mechanic and the Gardener: Laurence Le Shan, Holt, Rinehart and Winston, N.Y.

Befriending the Cancer Patient: Vera M. Naylor, Kershaw Publications, Liverpool.

I Want One Thing: Frances Horn, DeVorss and Co., P.O. Box 550, Marina del Rey, California.

The Macrobiotic Approach to Cancer: Kushi & East West Foundation. Avery Publishing Group inc., Wayne, New Jersey.

Attention of all oncologists is drawn to the recently formed British Psycho-social Oncological Group; secretary Dr. Margaret Watson, Faith Coutauld Unit, 123 Coldharbour Lane, London SE5 09NU.

Attention is also drawn to the following papers:

Psychological Response to Breast Cancer: Effect on Outcome. Greer, Morris and Pettingale: *Lancet*, Oct. 13, 1979. pp. 785 – 7.

Serum IGA and Emotional Expression in Breast Cancer Patients. Pettingale, Greer and Tee: Journ. Psychosomatic Res. vol. 21, pp. 395 – 9.

Prediagnostic Selenium and Risk of Cancer. Willett et al. *Lancet*, July 16, 1983, pp. 130 – 4.